Croner's Guide to MANAGING DISCIPLINE

Written and compiled by
Croner's Employment Law
Editorial Department

CRONER PUBLICATIONS LIMITED

Croner House, London Road,
Kingston upon Thames
Surrey KT2 6SR

Telephone: 081-547 3333

Printed by Whitstable Litho Ltd, Whitstable, Kent

Contents

Introduction

A glance at a dictionary or thesaurus can show that there is tremendous width of meaning in the word "discipline".

> *"Discipline" n. 1) (mental self-training) preparation, development, exercise, drilling, inculcation, training, regulation, self-discipline; 2) (a system of obedience)* — Syn. *conduct, regulation, drill, orderliness, restraint, limitation, curb, subordination to rules of conduct, indoctrination, brainwashing.*

From the latter it is small wonder that when the word "discipline" is used in its "heavy" sense it has negative connotations. However, there are amongst the dictionary definitions several more positive meanings for discipline than those associated with punishment, retribution and rigid compliance with the rules. It is these positive elements that are of most interest to people who manage staff in commerce, industry and other organisations. If these aspects of constructive discipline are properly understood trouble can be headed off before it actually starts to become an intractable situation.

Order

For instance, "order": this is usually seen as a desirable requirement in any organised group both by those in decision-making positions as well as those less influentially placed. Experience tells us that there is no management more severely criticised by its subordinates than one that is disorganised, lacking in direction and "can't get it together". Order is imposed by day to day rituals of work, ie the time of day during which work is to be performed, the routine job tasks that follow one after another and the methodical steps in completing the individual job tasks that build up the expectation of order in the lives of all working people.

One need only think of the unfortunate redundant employees who still take their train to work every day, even though they have nowhere to go, to realise the persuasiveness of routine and the comfort it gives.

In achieving order, getting the procedures right is an essential step so that matters of poor conduct, capability, etc can be dealt with in the right sequence and handled consistently by those in authority. The procedures can be a prop, taking away the anxieties of dealing with a variety of circumstances which in most organisations only occur occasionally. A large part of this book goes into detail about the operation of in-company disciplinary procedures and, particularly, using them with sensitivity to obtain a positive result.

Rules of Conduct

The idea of imposing "rules of conduct" particularly when they are put into writing and served up as "company rules" may not appeal to those with a liberal outlook. However, what they do not recognise is that all companies or organisations have accepted standards of behaviour from which individuals are not expected to depart. They are hardly ever written down or even spoken about but nevertheless they are there and apply to any new recruit to the organisation. These norms of conduct, dress, etc can vary from department to department and from company to company; the "laissez faire" standards adopted by one contrasting sharply with the almost Victorian strictness of others.

Sometimes it is the result of a particularly strong-minded individual (not always the person in charge) who helps to set departmental standards, especially for the new recruit. Take, for example, Hilda who doesn't like other people being late back from lunch because it is not fair on everyone (but particularly her because she doesn't have a break and has to answer all the telephones). Hilda sits and fumes in the corner making pointed remarks. No one likes to offend Hilda! (This is confirmed by everyone else in the department — from personal experience!) Everyone in the department is usually prompt in returning from lunch and loudly apologises if they are unavoidably detained. So the new recruit conforms to the norm. End of story.

Of course, some standards of behaviour develop which are not beneficial to the company or organisation, eg sleeping on the night shift or claiming unworked overtime as an accepted "turn a blind eye" practice. Such situations will need a management lead to establish new acceptable standards of behaviour.

From the informal setting of standards it is easy for organisations to graft on formal rules of conduct and with legal requirements in mind, there are good commonsense reasons for doing so. The codification of "works rules" or company rules outlining accepted standards of behaviour is a sensitive matter because the rules have to reflect custom and practice and be presented in an acceptable manner. The advantages of such an exercise are described later.

Codifying Company Rules

When starting the exercise of codifying rules for your organisation, it is certainly helpful to look at examples from other companies, but never forget that every organisation is unique and there may be particular rules that have grown up over time on an informal basis, perhaps even in individual departments. It is a good idea to involve all managers and supervisors in discussing the informal rules that they have made in their areas of responsibility before preparing the first draft. They are in the best possible position to know exactly how seriously they have treated any breach of such informal rules. It will be possible to rank these breaches into three categories:

Ranking breaches of company rules

- minor misconduct that merits an oral warning;
- more serious misconduct that will result in written warnings; and
- gross misconduct which will usually attract the ultimate penalty of dismissal.

It will be immediately apparent that different standards or degrees of laxity exist among managers and these discussions will considerably help to improve consistency throughout the organisation.

If company rules already exist there is nothing to lose — and a great deal to gain — by repeating the exercise periodically to review rules in the light of changed management, company policy and omissions that have become apparent since they were first prepared.

Remember also that in some circumstances it may be advisable for good business/commercial reasons to have different standards in different parts of the company. If this is the case it is absolutely essential that there is no doubt whatever in employees' minds as to which rules apply to them and, preferably, why the different standards have been adopted.

1 Discipline and the Law

By way of introduction to this chapter, there are two main points that should be stressed. First of all, the law does not say that companies must have disciplinary rules or policies, let alone prescribe what sort of procedures companies should adopt. What it does do, though, is to say that if companies dismiss an employee on grounds of misconduct, the dismissal will be unfair if the employer acted unreasonably in treating the misconduct as a sufficient reason for dismissal. This is backed up by a Code of Practice issued by the Advisory, Conciliation and Arbitration Service (ACAS) which sets out some ground rules on fairness and this applies to employers in much the same way as the Highway Code applies to motorists: breach of any of the Code's recommendations will have to be justified if an unfair dismissal claim goes to an industrial tribunal. The second point is that the law does say that if you have disciplinary rules, then details of them must be notified to employees, either directly or by referring them to a reasonably accessible document which specifies the rules.

The purpose of this book is not to provide legal advice on disciplinary matters but, in order that you can carry out the "man-management" part of your job effectively and, as far as possible, keep you and your company from running into trouble with industrial tribunals, this chapter looks at the main legal requirements on disciplinary practice and policies. The way that you can best handle the practical aspects of maintaining reasonable standards of conduct, while taking into account the legal requirements, is dealt with fully in pages 79 to 102.

Unfair Dismissal

Employees who work for at least 16 hours a week and have two years' service with a company have the right not to be unfairly dismissed. Part-time employees who work for at least eight but less than sixteen hours a week do not have this protection until they have been employed for five years.

People who are dismissed because of sex or race discrimination or because of trade union membership or activity gain protection from the law as soon as they join a company, so if employees with only a few months' service claimed that they were dismissed for one of those reasons, then it would be up to the employer to show that the dismissal was really on grounds of conduct or one of the other potentially "fair" reasons for dismissal.

Five Fair Reasons for Dismissal:

● capability or qualifications for the work employees are employed to do (this includes health);

● conduct;

● redundancy;

● continued employment would involve the employer or employee in breaking the law; or

● some other substantial reason justifying the dismissal of the employee.

Making a Claim

Any employees who are sacked, and have the necessary qualifying service, have the right to make a claim to an industrial tribunal that they have been unfairly dismissed. They make a claim on a special form (IT1) which they then send to the Central Office of Industrial Tribunals. They will send a copy of the form plus a form for the employer's defence — Notice of Appearance (IT3) — to the employer. If the claim cannot be settled through conciliation (which normally involves the employer making a payment to the ex-employee, but without any admission that the dismissal was unfair) then a tribunal hearing will be arranged, normally within about six weeks, but the delay between making the claim and the hearing taking place can vary enormously.

If the case does go to an industrial tribunal, the employer

has to prove that there was a fair reason for dismissal and then it is a question of whether it was reasonable to treat the employee's behaviour as a sufficient reason for dismissal: in other words, did the punishment fit the crime? The important point here will be the procedure that was followed before the dismissal. This is where the ACAS Code of Practice comes in as it sets out the sort of procedure that is considered to be reasonable.

The ACAS Code of Practice

The Code of Practice on Disciplinary Practice and Procedures in Employment was published by ACAS in 1977. The foreword to the Code states:

> *A failure on the part of any person to observe any provision of a Code of Practice shall not of itself render him liable to any proceedings; but in any proceedings before an industrial tribunal . . . any Code of Practice issued under this section shall be admissible in evidence, and if . . . relevant to any question arising in the proceedings it shall be taken into account in determining that question. (s.207(1), Trade Union and Labour Relations (Consolidation) Act 1992.)*

As the Code sets out the essential features of disciplinary procedures and recommendations as to how the procedure should be operated, it is a very important document. Copies of the Code can be obtained from ACAS. If all the Code's recommendations are not followed, it does not mean that a dismissal will be automatically unfair, though. It will then be for the employer to show that the procedure was fair in the circumstances of that particular company, and the particular case.

For instance, very small companies are not expected to have the same sophisticated procedures as would probably be found in a big multi-national business. Similarly, the sort of procedure that applies to a senior executive will often be different from that applied to a shop floor worker. The essential point is that the company behaves in a reasonable manner. Examples of the sort of behaviour expected from companies in different circumstances and for various kinds of misconduct are given on page 79.

What the Code Says

The main provisions of the Code relate to the essential features of the disciplinary procedure and its operation.

Disciplinary Procedures: The Main Points

Disciplinary procedures should:

- be in writing (this is dealt with below);

- specify to whom they apply — this seems to be commonsense but it is not unusual to find some employees who are quite sure that the rules really do not apply to them;

- provide the right for employees to hear the case against them and have the right to give their side of the story — particularly when somebody is apparently caught red-handed! They may well have a good reason. It may also be the case that misconduct is actually rooted in domestic or health problems so you will want to change your approach;

- give employees the right to be accompanied — it is important to establish in your own company whether this means that employees can have somebody else to speak for them or whether the person accompanying them is only there to "hold their hand". Another important point to settle is whether there are any restrictions on who the accompanying person can be. For instance, do you really want people to turn up with their solicitors?;

- ensure that there is a thorough investigation — this is a very important point and it is the lack of investigation that is most likely to lead to an unfair dismissal finding by a tribunal. If necessary, employees can be suspended for a brief period while the investigation is carried out, but the suspension should always be on full pay.

If, after the investigation, it is necessary to take formal disciplinary action against an employee, the Code suggests that the following steps should be taken:

(a) In the case of minor offences, the employee should be given a formal oral warning or, if the issue is more serious, there should be a written warning and the employee should be advised that the warning constitutes the first formal stage of the procedure.

(b) Further misconduct might warrant a final written warning.

(c) The final step might be disciplinary transfer or suspension without pay (but only if these are allowed for by an express or implied term of the contract of employment), or dismissal.
See Figure 1 at the end of this chapter.

The essential feature of warnings is that they should clearly spell out the nature of the misconduct, the improvement expected within a specified time and the consequences of failure to improve or further breaches of the rules — ie final written warning, dismissal, etc.

It is worth stressing here that the Code does not impose unreasonably high standards. It was not drafted in terms of the highest possible standard that companies could aim for. What it does do is to recommend the sort of practice that was being followed by the majority of companies even before the first legislation on unfair dismissal was introduced. It is a very useful document in that it sets out, in a straightforward way, commonsense rules for promoting order and fairness in the treatment of individuals.

Your Role at the Tribunal

In larger companies, the personnel or industrial relations manager/director is likely to handle the company's case before the tribunal and in smaller companies a solicitor might be retained. However, in almost all companies you, as a manager, are likely to have a crucial role to play as a witness. After all, you should be the person who first set the disciplinary procedure in motion, even if you were only actively involved in the early, informal stages, and you will be the person with the best knowledge of the employee, the conduct concerned and the steps that were taken to improve standards.

It is vital that you are in a position to give good, accurate evidence: not only will your company's defence at the tribunal depend on that in many cases, but so will your credibility with both your subordinates and the people above you in the organisation. Your success as a witness will depend on the way you handled the situation and the records you kept, and these points are dealt with in detail in later chapters of this book.

Putting it into Writing

The Employment Protection (Consolidation) Act 1978 (EPCA) says that all employees must be notified of any disciplinary rules that apply to them; either by giving them copies or telling them where they can be seen — in the personnel department, the supervisor's office, on company noticeboards, and so on — and, in the same way, they must be informed of who they can appeal to if they are dissatisfied with a disciplinary decision and how the appeal should be made.

It obviously makes a good deal of sense to have the rules and procedures in writing. It means that you know exactly what steps you can take, employees know where they stand, and union officials are better equipped to carry out their role. Written rules narrow any area of dispute and, if you've got to pull somebody up for bad timekeeping, performance or whatever, you do not want to get embroiled in an argument as to what the rules or procedures say or mean!

The best way of ensuring that employees are left in no doubt as to the meaning of rules and the standards expected of them is to incorporate this into the induction procedure which each new recruit to the company should go through, and ensure at this stage that they either have their own copies or know where to go to refresh their memories.

What Rules?

The rules set for employees in your company will depend on your particular circumstances and no one set of rules can ever be right for every organisation. There are, though, some good ground rules which are helpful, one of which is that, as far as possible the rules should be positive: do not keep saying "you must not . . .", say "you will . . .".

The conduct required of every employee takes on a special significance at work. The company's financial stability, reputation, ability to offer employment security and the provision of safe working conditions depends on each employee's individual performance.

An example of the sort of rules most likely to be found in companies is given below.

Sample Rules

1. **You are required to be punctual in observing times of work:**
— you are required to report punctually for work at the time stated in your terms and conditions of employment (shift rota posted on the noticeboard, etc);
— you must observe the stated lunch and tea breaks;
— it is a requirement that you do not leave your workplace before the finishing time stated in your terms and conditions statement;
— your working times can only be varied with the written authority of your immediate supervisor;
— special conditions of attendance (for other categories of staff) are set out in the company procedural manual or statement of terms and conditions.

2. **You are required to respect fellow employees:**
— do not intimidate, threaten or coerce fellow employees by using physical violence, improper language or other disorderly conduct;
— maintain sanitary conditions in washrooms and keep your workplace tidy;

- do not distribute unauthorised pamphlets or literature;
- do not place unauthorised documents on the company noticeboard or remove or deface those documents placed with the authority of management;
- do not gamble on company premises;
- you must follow all reasonable instructions of supervisors and managers.

3. **You are required to respect both the property of the company and your fellow employees:**
- do not abuse, deface or wilfully damage company property;
- do not use company telephones for personal calls except in case of emergency;
- do not accept personal telephone calls except in cases of emergency;
- company vehicles may only be used by authorised employees;
- use company property only for company activities. Do not take company property for personal use either on or off company premises;
- use your work time only for company responsibilities. Do not use work time for personal projects or activities.

4. **You are required to protect personnel and company facilities:**
- smoke only in those areas where smoking is permitted;
- do not carry any form of weapon, explosive or inflammable substance on to the company premises;
- you are required to follow safe, normal work procedures and use only the equipment which you are authorised to use;
- always make sure that the safety guards provided are working correctly and are correctly positioned;
- in event of fire or other alarms follow standing instructions and the orders given by your supervisor or manager, immediately and in an orderly manner.

5. **You are required to be free from the influence of alcohol or drugs:**

— do not bring alcohol to company premises or consume alcohol except in the case of organised occasions previously authorised by . . . . .;

— do not use, be under the influence of or bring to the company premises any form of narcotic other than those prescribed for your personal use by a registered physician.

6. **You are required to be truthful and accurate when completing company documents and records:**

— this requirement includes completion of all personnel forms, medical records, leave requests and other company forms;

— it is contrary to company rules under all circumstances to falsify the time or attendance records of a fellow employee or encourage a fellow employee to take such action on your behalf.

7. **You are required to comply with the company's procedural handbook, copies of which can be seen (on company noticeboards, in the supervisor's office, etc):**

— such written procedures concerning employee expenses, cars, holidays, pension, benefits, etc; which are circulated on a personal basis;

— it is the responsibility of each employee to be aware of the contents of such procedures which might affect their working conditions.

8. **You are required to treat information acquired during the course of your job as confidential:**

— do not convey to any person not in the company's employment any document relating to the business of the company except those published for distribution to the general public;

— do not fill in or discuss any trading, marketing or financial surveys of any nature unless authorised in writing by a director of the company;

- do not disclose information concerning company products, product development or development plans except that which is published for circulation to the general public;

- do not discuss or disclose any matters concerning financial operations or trading practices to any unauthorised person within the company or to persons outside the company.

Breaches of these requirements will be dealt with under the company's disciplinary procedure as the circumstances require.

Common Law

Another aspect of the law to be taken into account is "common law" — that is, judge-made law rather than Acts of Parliament. For the purposes of this book, it is common law as it relates to contracts of employment. An employer who breaks an important term of an employee's contract will be in fundamental breach of the contract and the employee would be entitled to leave — with or without notice — and, providing he or she had the necessary qualifying service, make a claim to an industrial tribunal of unfair (constructive) dismissal. Alternatively, the employee could remain in the job but claim damages from the county courts in respect of the employer's breach.

Contractual Rules and Procedures

On page 10 we mentioned the importance of having the rules and procedures in writing and ensuring that copies are given to all employees. Some employers do this by incorporating them into the contract of employment. This is fair enough in many ways but there are two potential problem areas:

● unless the full procedure is used for new employees who do not come up to standard, when they are dismissed they could get damages from the county courts for the breach, which would normally be equivalent to their wages for the period it would have taken to operate the procedure; and

14

- because contracts can only be varied with the agreement of both parties, any changes could only be made with the consent of the workforce or, where there is good reason for making the change, by giving the employees proper notice to terminate their employment and offering immediate re-engagement on the new terms.

These problems can be overcome to some extent by including in the contract the right of management to change the rules and/or procedures and the right to shorten or vary the procedure at their discretion, although this may not do much to heighten employees' faith in the company's fairness.

Constructive Dismissal

Another aspect of common law to be considered is that it automatically implies into employees' contracts such terms as:

- a duty on employers to maintain the employment relationship;
- a duty of good faith; and
- a duty to pay salary/wages.

This means that employers who break any of these terms by, for instance, showing that they no longer have confidence in the employee (without good reason) or suspending an employee without pay (when there is no contractual provision allowing this course of action) will be in breach of contract and so the employee could resign and claim constructive dismissal.

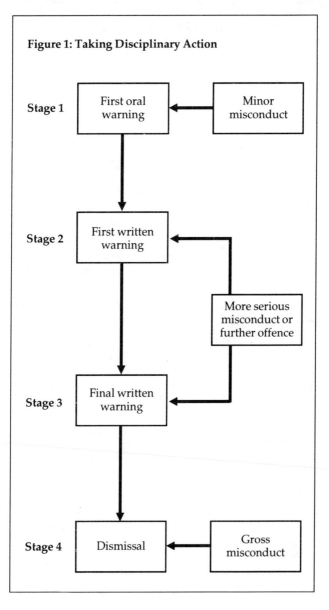

Figure 1: Taking Disciplinary Action

Stage 1: First oral warning ← Minor misconduct

Stage 2: First written warning ← More serious misconduct or further offence

Stage 3: Final written warning ← More serious misconduct or further offence

Stage 4: Dismissal ← Gross misconduct

2 The Need for Discipline

It may seem better not to worry too much about maintaining a reasonable degree of order at work, and there are a variety of reasons often put forward for this: it would spoil the atmosphere; it only causes legal problems; people work better if they are left alone; it would upset the unions, and so on. These arguments can seem quite compelling, and it is worth examining them more fully, but the overriding point to remember is that the word "discipline" does not mean managers must act like sergeant majors. What we are talking about is, in the words of the ACAS Code of Practice on Discipline (see page 7):

> *Disciplinary rules and procedures are necessary for promoting fairness and order in the treatment of individuals and in the conduct of industrial relations. They also assist an organisation to operate effectively. Rules set standards of conduct at work; procedure helps to ensure that the standards are adhered to and also provides a fair method of dealing with alleged failures to observe them.*

It is this definition that forms the keynote of this book: it is the job of managers at all levels to ensure that the part of the organisation that is within their control operates effectively, and that their behaviour towards employees who do not observe standards is fair.

Bear in mind that when we talk about disciplinary action, we are talking about two separate things:

- informal action — somebody comes in late, or does sloppy work, and you pull them up about it on the spot or, at a more serious level, you call them into your office and give them an informal warning; and

●   formal action — this will normally follow on from informal action or will be the first step in serious misconduct cases and this really means that the employee could be on the road to dismissal.
See Figure 2 at the end of this chapter.

The rest of this chapter concentrates on looking at the reasons why all companies need rules and procedures that are known and understood by everyone.

Upsetting the Unions

When companies recognise trade unions, an important part of the job of shop stewards is to represent their members when disciplinary action is being taken against them, and there is obviously scope for conflict with the union in this area. This, though, should be no reason for backing away from taking disciplinary action. There is nothing more likely to cause trouble than allowing people to get away with things over a period then, when an employee finally goes too far, coming the heavy hand.

It is unreasonable in most companies to expect that shop stewards will want to become involved with any activities that seem to range them on the side of management in disciplinary procedures, but if they are brought into the procedure automatically, as representatives of union members, and the procedure adopted is fair and is applied consistently, there is no need in the vast majority of cases for disciplinary action to turn into conflict.

Similarly, unions have a useful role to play in helping to formulate and review procedures; such an involvement will lend credence to the fact that the procedure exists to ensure that suspected breaches of discipline are handled fairly.

If disciplinary action of any sort has to be taken against a shop steward, then obviously a very careful approach has to be adopted to avoid the action being seen as an attack on the union itself, which can obviously lead to serious industrial relations problems. No formal action should be taken until the circumstances have been discussed with either a full-time union official or a more senior union representative.

Spoiling a Friendly Atmosphere

It is often the case that managers who take the line that to introduce formal disciplinary procedures would spoil the atmosphere, lead to reduced productivity, etc, are already applying such good standards that the lack of formal procedures has never been a problem, since difficulties have always been resolved in the informal stages. This, though, begs the question of what you do when faced with an employee who is totally intractable: who will not come into work on time, or who will not stop disrupting other people.

This sort of behaviour will usually have one of two results: either the other employees will see that employee getting away with murder and so will relax their own standards, or they will become very angry with the manager for allowing the person to "get away with it". Neither of these situations makes for a friendly atmosphere and, of course, a good manager will not let the situation drift too far. What, though, should be done? No matter how fair the procedure you adopt might seem to you, if it comes as a complete break from normal practice — and so from the employee's expectations — trouble will result.

Another difficulty is that action may well be taken in the heat of the moment, and such action is more likely than not to depart from the rules of fairness and natural justice. The same considerations apply when the philosophy is that people are better left on their own. They are, so long as you can rely on them, but you could still meet with one intractable employee.

"One of the Workers"

One of the most difficult situations to cope with is promotion to manager of your own department. Overnight, you have to change from being a workmate to being responsible for order and output.

This transition can be made much easier if your company has well-defined rules and procedures: without opting out of your new responsibilities, you can point out to the people you are managing that both you and they know the rules: they know the procedure for enforcing them and they must appreciate that you have got to stick to them otherwise the people above you in the organisation could start using that same procedure on you for falling down on the job! Without any guidelines to begin with your life will be much more difficult.

The Legal Problems

It may be tempting to decide that to avoid getting involved with the law you will back out of the whole discipline scene, either by doing nothing more than giving a good roasting, or by passing on the problems to your boss. In some cases, your own company's policy might be that no formal steps can be taken by you without having further authority: that's fine, but if discipline is your responsibility then you are going to run into a lot of problems. Once your own subordinates realise that you are not prepared to take any action yourself they could well make your life a misery, and you won't exactly endear yourself to your boss by constantly insisting that he or she does your dirty work.

Nobody is suggesting that, just because there are laws on unfair dismissal, you must think or act like a solicitor.

Remember that the law only expects companies to act in a fair and reasonable way. It demands no more, on the whole, than is necessary for the sake of maintaining good relations between management and workforce.

Developing Employees

The most positive aspect of discipline is "development". Indisciplined employees will not give the best of themselves and their performance will be below that of which they are capable. Their indiscipline is met with complaint and reprimand by those in authority over them, and often enough their fellow workers as well who see them as abusing the situation or creating waves for everyone else by forcing the manager to take notice and tighten things up. The working relationship between those in authority and the employees they are responsible for is one of swings and roundabouts with most of the participants opting for a quiet life when the crunch comes. More often than not inertia is the response to potential conduct problems that could be recognised at quite an early stage, but remain untackled by managers; possibly because the procedures are not there or, if they are there, they are just not used until the "last straw" situation arrives. All chances of salvaging the employees and making them valued contributors to the organisation have gone. Those young and inexperienced recruits whose knowledge of work is limited, members of the "awkward squad", the sly, rule stretchers and the "you owe me a living" types soon find that there is an irresistible force propelling them "down the road" with their cards in hand.

Not many tears will be shed for the worst of them but there are often those who would, but for the lack of timely action by their manager, still be doing a useful job.

Initiating such remedial action must be seen as a major responsibility for anyone who is in charge of staff, be they section leader, manager or entrepreneur, because even in a recession no one can afford to waste talent (not to mention the recruitment and training costs involved). The best managers know that in the majority of cases the right word at the right time to an apparently erring employee is all that is required and counselling will often be a more satisfactory method of dealing with matters than formal disciplinary procedures. If in the end the formal procedures have to be used, the unpleasant legal consequences of unfair dismissal can usually be avoided; managers have been seen to have acted fairly in giving the employee "a good length of rope" before dismissal and the employee will leave feeling, "well, they did give me every chance".

The Financial Costs

Finally, it has to be said that the financial costs incurred by the company when managers neglect their "discipline" role can be enormous, whether the costs have to be counted in terms of lost production — due to absenteeism, lateness, lack of skill or downright idleness — and, in the case of dismissals which could have been avoided if appropriate remedial action had been taken at the right time, in the cost of advertising for, recruiting and training new employees.

Conclusion

Simply the fact that you have, and work by, rules and procedures for dealing with misconduct will not, by itself, smooth out the difficulties you will inevitably have to face at some time. Hopefully, though, you will now accept that there is a need to use the procedures, and the remainder of this book is aimed at giving practical advice and tips to help you deal with the wide variety of the problems that fall under the "discipline" umbrella.

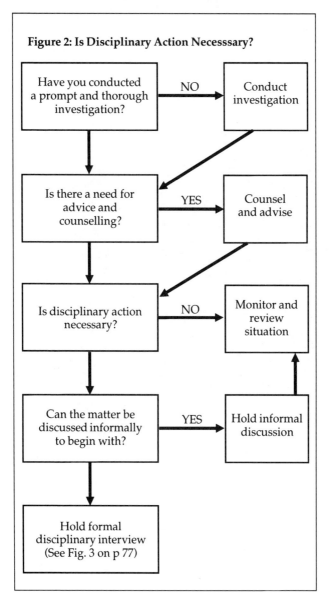

Figure 2: Is Disciplinary Action Necesssary?

Have you conducted a prompt and thorough investigation? — NO → Conduct investigation

Is there a need for advice and counselling? — YES → Counsel and advise

Is disciplinary action necessary? — NO → Monitor and review situation

Can the matter be discussed informally to begin with? — YES → Hold informal discussion

Hold formal disciplinary interview (See Fig. 3 on p 77)

3 The Role of the Manager

It is not within the scope of this chapter to enter into a detailed discussion of the role of the manager. It is a very complex job and we will only be concentrating on the manager's practical and effective approach to maintaining standards within his or her department. Firstly, let us pose the problem: who is the manager?

Everyone working with staff who can decide the priority, quality and quantity of work that those staff undertake must consider themselves as having first line responsibility for discipline. That affects all levels of management including managing directors (for their secretary, personal assistant, etc), branch managers (for their administration staff, departmental managers etc), section leaders in a factory, and even the senior typist who is in charge of the office junior. Sooner or later an issue arises in the best run departments which requires putting an end to unacceptable behaviour or emphasising the proper standards of job performance.

The fact that someone has to take responsibility for discipline is the crux of the problem. "Henry never gets things right and is a terrible timekeeper, perhaps the Personnel Department will have to have a word with him!" This is shifting the responsibility from where it quite correctly lies and in the process can actually damage the relationship between the manager and the employee. Too frequently employees are heard to say "Why couldn't he or she have told me that my work wasn't all right? Why did he or she have to involve someone else?"

To be really effective, the first informal steps should always be taken by the employee's immediate manager who hopefully knows the employee quite well and will be the person who is immediately aware of any improvements as a result of their talk.

Most organisations delegate the authority to give informal reprimands to the employee's immediate manager so that minor everyday problems of conduct and job performance can be dealt with swiftly.

Most managers would say that they don't have the time to involve themselves in the personal problems of those they manage and would not wish to see that aspect of their job assume greater significance, especially if there is a personnel department. Many managers would say that it just wasn't their business to enquire into the personal life of those they manage. Indeed they would argue that just the problems of maintaining production, whether it be on the factory floor, the typing pool or in the executive suite, is all they have time to do. However, managers of staff who do take this approach cannot expect to be as effective as those who do take responsibility because their decisions do not take into account relevant information and are often wildly inappropriate. You need only look at the welter of tribunal cases to see how some of their decisions have come expensively to grief.

It is not necessary to go overboard; it is simply a question of asking if there are any personal problems preying on employees' minds that may be affecting their attitude to work. An individual's personal circumstances do have a large bearing on job performance. (Particularly look out for the previously adequate employee who dramatically falls off in performance.) Very often solutions occur as a result of these enquiries, ie a week's compassionate leave, a change of department or job, the short term change of starting time to allow aged parents to be cared for until a more permanent arrangement can be made, etc. Such action can sort out the problem effectively whilst formal disciplinary warnings alone would have exacerbated the situation by increasing the pressure on an already pressurised employee.

Concern should not Prevent Action

Knowing the personal circumstances in which employees find themselves does not prevent disciplinary action being taken in the end: employers are not required to go on sympathising indefinitely with the employee with personal problems that spill over into job performance. There comes a time when the employer must demand that standards are kept regardless of these personal problems so that the business or the smooth operation of the department does not suffer. Consequently, it is important for the employee to know where and when the line will be drawn and this can be done more formally if the informal approach does not work.

Finding all Relevant Facts

Finding out if there are personal problems in mitigation is only one aspect of the manager's vital role in gathering the facts of the case together before deciding what to do. The most important part of the exercise is getting "genned up" about the complaint you are going to make to the employee so that you can combat worthless excuses and state the complaint with some precision. For instance, is the work performance really worse than the rest of the department (what data supports such a contention); what does the analysis of the attendance records show; is the bulk of the lost time a result of a stay in hospital which has now corrected the problem or is it unexplained absence which amazingly always falls on a Monday or a Friday? In other words, make sure of your facts before tackling the employee concerned and make a note of the points that should be covered so that no relevant aspect is missed.

Consistency

As if to prove that working "through" people is not easy there is another problem inherent in the role of the supervisor: consistency. It is only human to have preferences; to tolerate a little more from one employee whilst coming down like a ton of bricks on another, but to do it blatantly is always a dangerous practice and does nothing to build up trust in the manager's fairmindedness. It simply does not pay to have favourites so far as discipline is concerned. Consistency also means consistency over a period of time. With some managers, control is lacking and slack timekeeping becomes custom and practice in their department. Other "nodded-at" practices develop through sheer lethargy, eg unworked overtime may be allowed, arrangements to slow the machine's output to create overtime, etc, may be condoned over a long period of time.

Now, to tighten up and change these working practices it is necessary to give ample warning and explanation as to why it is no longer an acceptable practice. The new requirement, ie where the line is now drawn, should be stated precisely so that no one is in doubt and a clear indication should be given that disciplinary action will be taken if that line is disregarded. Just to start dishing out warnings and reprimands without making it clear that "it's a new ball game" would be quite inappropriate and of course employers who recognise a trade union will in many cases have to consult with the union and perhaps buy out the practice before taking action. So, major changes in working practices in a department ought to be properly discussed with other managers who may at a later stage find themselves being involved.

The Manager's Responsibilities for Discipline: Four key areas

- establishing and maintaining standards of acceptable conduct and work performance of the employees for whom direct responsibility is held;

- consistently upholding these standards, as far as possible, without fear or favour (unless there is a good reason for adopting another view of the matter or taking different action);

- halting unacceptable behaviour at the outset with an appropriate word at the right time, ie too much talking, untidy work, general messing about, bad language, etc, and dealing with aspects of conduct and performance that deteriorate over a period of time;

- the proper investigation and formulation of the complaint concerning poor conduct or job performance prior to taking the employee to task about it informally.

There is a great deal to be said for managers trying to establish an agreed approach for dealing with minor misconduct, poor performance, etc, within an organisation. Even talking over a problem with others similarly placed in charge of employees, rather than struggling alone, can provide an important chance to pool experience and agree standards which are consistent throughout the organisation.

Giving informal warnings or counselling can be a difficult situation for anyone, even a manager with many years of experience, and the following section of the book deals with some of the pitfalls and strategies that might help when tackling an employee "face to face".

4   Informal Action is Important

The informal warning is probably the most important step in the whole disciplinary process because this is where the best chances exist to get the employee to conform and perform correctly. It is also a step that is easy to convince yourself to avoid because of the fear of mishandling.

There really are no standard formulae for handling people; sensitivity, applied commonsense and knowing what must be achieved by the confrontation is all that managers have to rely on. Flexibility of approach is essential so that account can be taken of the situations and personalities involved.

Additionally, employment legislation, and the involvement of unions, may result in many employers and their responsible staff saying that they are frightened to take any action to pull up the employees who behave badly — as one person said, he was frightened to give anyone a good telling-off in case he inadvertently constructively dismissed them!

Clearly, if there is a reluctance to get involved in "face to face" disciplinary situations it is because managers want to know "what can I say?" "what do I do when they react?", "if all goes horribly wrong how can I recover my position without complete loss of face?" "how far can I go?" and "what is my legal position?" It is the answers to these and many more questions we hope to provide.

The first step is deciding whether any approach should be made to the employee — is it a trivial matter and if not, how serious is it and has it occurred before?

Checklist: Should Action be Taken?

● Is the matter trivial and worth overlooking or must informal or formal disciplinary action be taken early on to prevent recurrence?

Things to Bear in Mind

— Will the conduct be potentially dangerous or lead to financial loss?

— Is it conduct that shows a deeper disrespect for those in authority?

— Is it conduct that encourages others to copy and therefore get out of control?

— Are the errors in performance fundamental to the successful performance of the employee's job?

— Is it conduct in breach of a rule or regulation that is not normally enforced?

— Is it conduct that irritates or offends other workers?

If the answer to any of these questions is yes, then action must be taken to correct it.

● Has any informal or formal action been taken before? If it has, this will determine at what level you start taking disciplinary action. Check personnel records and any personal record kept of informal disciplinary action.

● Formulate precisely what the complaint is, check the facts and get the evidence together. (This won't take long in most circumstances but, in some cases, may involve taking statements from employees who saw the incidents and other detailed investigation. Where this is going to be a lengthy process the employee concerned should be suspended on full pay.)

● If necessary check company disciplinary procedure and consult with the personnel department and immediate superior before deciding whether informal action is necessary or, because of the serious nature of the matter, a direct entry into formal disciplinary action is desirable.

On-the-Job Reprimand

If it is a clear cut situation involving minor misconduct such as inattention to work, too much talking, untidy work, etc, then often an informal oral warning can be given immediately. This is quite distinct from a chivvying remark or giving supplementary instructions: it indicates that the limits of acceptable behaviour have been reached.

It is important that the warning is given carefully. The purpose is not to humiliate employees in front of their fellow workers as this encourages an aggressive response which may be difficult to handle; others may be tempted to get involved and in an instant the matter can get out of control. Try to settle it in private. Always avoid abusiveness and do not personalise the warning. Withering sarcasm is also very destructive especially to younger employees. Most employees, if approached in this manner, "turn off" — they cease to listen to anything that is said to them — they do not participate in the disciplinary process and the chance of successfully obtaining their co-operation and respect is reduced.

It goes without saying that at all times getting involved in arguments is taboo. If one starts to develop, just listen. Then reassert your position when the employee has run out of steam. Physical contact should also be avoided — even a guiding outstretched arm can be misinterpreted.

Although these interviews are usually unplanned and carried out in less than ideal circumstances somehow the manager has to find the time and a suitable place to deal immediately with the problem.

To assist in these objectives, a useful guide to follow is outlined on the next page.

Other situations can be more complicated and should ideally be given a more lengthy treatment even though the matter is being dealt with on the informal level. Thoroughness does pay off big dividends.

How to Handle an On-the-Job Reprimand

- if you have lost your cool, indicate that you will deal with the matter shortly and go and calm down;

- call the employee to a place out of earshot and view of others. If more than one employee is involved explain that you wish to see them one at a time. Emphasise that the same thing will be said to each person involved. Avoid being put under pressure by being outnumbered.

- some managers find preliminary calming down tactics like offering a cup of tea a useful way of "heading off" an aggressive reaction. Find time to compose yourself and allow the employee's mood to decline and wariness to subside. Sending out for the union representative is often a way to do this if your company's disciplinary procedure requires the attendance of the representative at any disciplinary interview. Do not forget to ask if they want a friend (employed by the company) present whilst you are talking to them. Most will decline;

- explain in measured tones what they have done and why it is not acceptable or sensible. Ask if there is any explanation they wish to offer;

- try always to observe the normal social courtesies. Try to avoid raising your voice and be as brief and as clear as possible;

- try to avoid tension in body posture, facial expression and your voice. Keep eye contact with employees to emphasise the things you are saying in a relaxed way. Your face should register seriousness of purpose because verbal reprimands given whilst smiling or joking are not effective;

- summarise the situation at the end of the interview. Make sure the employees are told that the conversation must be treated as an informal verbal warning; make a note of the incident.

First, we shall look at organising disciplinary interviews which in principle remain much the same at both the formal and informal levels, including how to cope if things start to go wrong and some strategies to adopt depending on the type of disciplinary problem that is being dealt with.

Organising Disciplinary Interviews

Problems such as lateness, absence, poor performance and attitude develop over a period of time and when dealing with these issues, more often than not it is the manager who picks the time and place to tackle the employee. This initial approach should be made at an informal level in the first instance. Because the manager is initiating the action there is little excuse for poor preparation and investigation which form the vital preliminary steps before a disciplinary interview.

Timing

Setting the time of that interview can sometimes be important. If emotional scenes or other difficulties are anticipated, set the time for late afternoon so that the employee can leave as normal and not involve anyone else on the premises. Similarly, Friday ought to be the popular day for disciplinary interviews so that employees have the weekend to think over the implications of the discussion. This is, of course, a difficult day for some people because wages are paid and time may be difficult to find. You may also have to arrange for the recognised trade union steward to be present if it is a requirement of the company disciplinary procedure. Remember that if a dispute arises over the facts of the incident you may have to call in witnesses to support your allegations. (This is more likely to happen in serious misconduct matters which are dealt with at the formal levels of procedure.)

Surroundings

Do not ignore the physical setting of the interview. Beg, borrow or steal an office or place where you will not be disturbed — somewhere quiet, with available seating. Leave instructions to prevent phone calls being put through to you. The employee must be aware that a special effort is being directed towards him or her. With employees who are on first name terms and who mix socially with those in charge of them, it can be difficult for the manager to "distance" him or herself, to adopt a concerned but detached attitude when disciplining employees and there is a temptation to do nothing until the last straw. This means that the manager loses his or her temper and an argument may result. Dismissals that occur in this way are usually unfair, with all the financial liability that is involved.

"Distancing"

The important point is to show the employee that you are putting on your "authority hat" — "distancing" yourself. This can be done by using a more formal way of speaking. "Peter, I must ask you to come to my office, I would like to have a serious talk with you." If you maintain eye contact as well, Peter will be in no doubt that you are being serious and will understand that you are going to take him to task about something.

Surprisingly, such pull-ups often come as a relief to employees who realise they have been living dangerously. In summary, do not wait until too much damage has been done; deal with the problem before it gets to the stage where dismissal is the only possible outcome. It is only human nature to see how far you can go before someone blows the whistle so do not think that relationships must become permanently damaged as a result.

Useful Hints on Face to Face Meetings

Having ushered the employee into an office (some thought should have been given to the setting so that the seating arrangement has been sorted out beforehand) invite the employee to sit down. The serious intent of the conversation will be reinforced by the manager taking a seat behind a table or desk. Never use psychological ploys like making the employee face into the light whilst you remain in the shadow or keeping him or her standing whilst you are seated. There is no need to use MI5 tactics and at this informal level there is no need for any witnesses.

Make sure that you can hear each other easily, so do not sit too far apart; make sure you are not constantly interrupted with people coming in, and if this happens apologise to the employee for the intrusion. Preliminary tactics discussed on page 34 help to compose both the manager and the employee and help to set the scene for constructive conversations. Observe all the normal courtesies: storming about the office or hammering on the desk with your fist is almost always counterproductive. The whole purpose of the interview is to tell the employee, in measured tones, without losing your temper or raising your voice, the reason for your dissatisfaction. If the employee starts vociferously to defend him or herself (after all, attack is the best form of defence) — listen. You do not lose face by listening but you do if you start to browbeat and shout the employee down.

It is useful to have notes on all the points you wish to talk to the employee about, insist that you wish to go through them point by point and then hear what the employee has to say about each one. Make it clear that you are not dissatisfied with everything: some aspects of performance may be very good whilst others, for example, timekeeping may be appalling. You should take the opportunity to give praise as well as constructive criticism. This will confirm to the employee that the discussion will be a useful and a constructive one in which encouragement will be given and good behaviour will be rewarded. The employee will be more inclined to co-operate and will not mentally "shut-off" and stop listening.

Documents

If there are any data or documents, eg production output figures, attendance, timekeeping records, letters of complaint from customers, etc, then show them to the employee and explain your interpretation of them. Give the employee an indication of what you think is going wrong and why he or she is falling below standard. Here, you must seize the opportunity to get the employee to offer explanations or reasons why he or she is failing to reach the expected standard. Encourage the search for these reasons by suggesting some yourself.

Interview Should not be One-sided

Get the employee to speak — a disciplinary interview is a two-way process not just a one-sided harangue. See if there are any personal problems that are having an unsettling effect and may account for the below-standard behaviour. If the employee will not discuss these problems with you, offer the chance to speak to the personnel officer or another manager. If there is still a reluctance, then you can only explain that if personal problems are relevant you will not be able to take them into account when assessing the situation if they cannot be discussed.

Assessing the Employee's Excuses

You will have to consider what validity any of the reasons given have, because they may be sufficient for you to reconsider your actions in giving an informal warning. This is another function of the disciplinary interview, to ensure that all relevant information is assessed before the warning is given. If there is any doubt about the appropriateness of the warning — don't give it. The disciplinary interview does help to avoid embarrassing mistakes. Sometimes a totally different set of facts are brought to light by the employee. You will have to check them out if there is any likelihood that they are true, eg an employee may have been given a different set of instructions by another manager which he or she has acted upon, or the down time on their machine has affected output and this was beyond their control (you may find it necessary to suspend the interview and resume later after these revelations have been checked).

You must consider: do the reasons actually account for the poor performance? Were the matters complained of within the employee's control or the fault of the organisation or someone else? Do not be afraid to tell the employee that their reasons are substantial and that you will be taking no further action except to try to iron out the problem at source. This is another main objective of the disciplinary meeting: to eliminate the problem, not just to punish the employee.

If on the other hand you find that the reasons given are

merely an excuse, then you should say so plainly. Do not give the impression that you have accepted an excuse when you think it is irrelevant or implausible. Do not be angry at prevarication, it is perfectly natural to try to excuse yourself when confronted.

Searching for Solutions

The next step in the interview is to reinforce to the employee, whatever the excuses, that the situation is unacceptable and ask him or her what they are going to do about improving their conduct or performance. Of course, you will also consider if there are any steps the company can take to help the situation, eg temporary changes to the hours of work, retraining, etc.

Search for the solution together and try to get the employee's commitment to a remedial course of action because in the long term his or her continued employment will depend on its success.

Before sending the employee back to work draw the interview to a close and summarise what has been talked about under the following headings:

● the complaint and the reasons why this is not an acceptable standard of behaviour/performance;

● the reasons given by the employee for this failure and any arrangements or remedial action agreed, including any time period over which matters will be reviewed;

● what the next steps will be if there is no improvement (refer to the company's formal disciplinary procedures, if there are any).

It may be necessary to discuss any special arrangements with senior managers first, and if the go-ahead is given send some written confirmation to the employee (especially if they involve a temporary change of contractual terms such as hours of work or special leave of absence). Make sure all the conditions attached to such an arrangement are specified, ie length of time, with or without pay, etc, in writing.

Things May Go Wrong

It would be too much to expect that every disciplinary interview will go smoothly. Though, surprisingly, most will if the problems have been caught at an early stage. Some particular problems encountered are given below.

Emotional Reactions

Some employees present real problems to their manager in a disciplinary interview by reacting in a very emotional manner. This might take the form of tears: these might be entirely genuine but they shouldn't prevent the interview from being completed. Offer to get a drink of water, hand over a paper handkerchief and tell the employee to "dry your eyes and we'll continue when you have composed yourself (however long it takes)".

When the employee realises that the situation cannot be avoided he or she is usually prepared to continue. If the tears break out again use the same tactic, or perhaps, if the employee is considerably agitated suspend the interview until the following day. Whatever happens, once started, the interview must be completed. Equally, the reaction might be more aggressive: physical violence might be threatened. This should be dealt with in the way suggested below (Gross Misconduct During the Interview) if the threat is real and immediate. However, if you believe that the threat is groundless and is just another symptom of an emotional reaction, it may be more effective to adjourn the meeting for ten minutes or so, and make it clear that an apology will be necessary when the meeting resumes.

Involvement of Union Representatives

In companies where recognised shop stewards are involved at the informal stages, the degree to which they participate depends on custom and practice. Ideally, one should aim to confine them to the role of observer and allow them to give advice to their members outside the door or in another office. If the steward is going to be present and is likely to be articulate on the employee's behalf make sure another member of the management team is present to observe the proceedings and provide advice.

Gross Misconduct During the Interview

Sometimes the response can be explosive: cups of coffee can be poured over the interviewing manager, fists can start to fly or the language deteriorates to the extent that it is intolerable. If physical violence is offered then, providing it was unprovoked by the interviewer, it should be dealt with as a gross misconduct situation. First, restrain the employee, call for help if necessary, then suspend the employee and send him or her off the company premises with instructions to return the next day for the matter to be considered. Then arrange for a senior manager to review the situation next day at an interview with the employee and decide whether or not to dismiss. Many company rules provide for insubordinate behaviour and bad language to be treated as acts of gross misconduct, and the same sort of procedure should be adopted as that stated below. Even if managers do have the authority to dismiss, as they cannot be considered disinterested parties, it is better to have someone uninvolved to adjudicate on the matter after a period of suspension. Usually, when the employee returns, he or she is ready to apologise and the interview can be completed. It is always sensible to allow employees to climb down gracefully when they have done things in the heat of the moment and a final warning would be appropriate punishment, though much depends on what they actually did when they were angry.

Storming Out

Getting employees into the interview is easy but having them stay and co-operate to the end is much harder. Once again employees use avoidance tactics. You should make it clear to employees that if they leave the office it is in defiance of your reasonable instructions, that you will take it further, to a senior manager, and dismissal may result. If that doesn't work, say that you are suspending the interview until the next working day when they have calmed down and then you will continue where you left off. If they do not think they should be reprimanded tell them of the right of appeal (according to the company's appeal procedure) to a senior manager. The reconvened interview should then take place with the senior manager present.

Don't lose heart, because these situations are rare and are usually the result of a volatile employee being tackled too late. It must be clear to anyone that an employee acting so unreasonably is putting him or herself into an even worse position from which they cannot win.

Solicitors and Other Ploys

The ways of dealing with the problems given above are not the only solutions neither are they the only disruptive situations that can happen. Many managers are thoroughly discomfited when employees demand the presence of their solicitors or a copy of their contract of employment (a statement must be received within 13 weeks of starting employment and very often it is overlooked), or younger workers may demand that one of their parents attends. Such positions are taken so that disciplinary action appears to be enormously difficult and full of unseen problems and the manager backs down as a result.

Actually, the answers are quite simple. In general, there is no right for employees to call their solicitors to be in attendance at disciplinary meetings and one is on fairly safe ground to refuse such a request. Similarly, parents have no specific right to attend unless they are parties to an apprenticeship contract. (There are, of course, situations when it is a good idea to involve parents, especially when formal disciplinary procedures are being used.) Contracts of employment rarely have any bearing on the disciplinary requirements, minimum production requirements, etc, but this does not mean that a manager cannot quite validly take someone to task for failing to reach a reasonable standard.

Monitoring the Success of Informal Disciplinary Action

If a period of assessment or retraining, etc, has been arranged then allow this period to expire before deciding whether the required standards have been reached or if formal disciplinary action will now be necessary.

It is always sensible to make some effort to give special attention to an employee during this review period, both to encourage and to give guidance. Try to give them the feeling that you wish them to succeed in reaching the standards required and you aren't going to treat them like social pariahs because you are unhappy with some aspect of their job performance or embarrassed at having to take them to task over it.

If the necessary improvement has not been made then it is time for a formal disciplinary interview. Check your company procedures to see who has the authority to give this warning; it is usually a departmental manager or general manager. You will need to ensure that he or she is alerted to the need to take action.

Note the dates when review periods come to an end in your diary and ensure that you reappraise the situation honestly when the time arrives. If the employee has made satisfactory improvement then say so. If it is only qualified improvement and you would like to give a little longer, once again, tell the employee and explain why there are still problem areas in job performance or conduct.

A checklist summarising the main points to bear in mind when conducting an informal disciplinary interview follows on the next page.

Checklist: Informal Disciplinary Interview

● **Preliminary Steps**

— Have you got the facts at your fingertips?

— Have you obtained all the relevant written data and documents?

— Have you defined precisely what your complaint is?

— Have you thought of the excuses that might be offered and would they form a reasonable defence against your complaint? Investigate.

— Have you made brief notes of the matters you intend to raise to prompt your memory and to make sure you do not leave anything out?

● **Physical Organisation of the Interview**

— Is there a quiet place, out of earshot of others, where the employee can be spoken to in private?

— Is there adequate seating?

— Have instructions been left that no one should disturb the meeting whether by phone or physical intrusion?

— Does the company disciplinary procedure require the recognised trade union representative to be present? If that is the case, ensure he or she is invited to the meeting.

— Has tea or coffee been organised to help put the employee at ease?

— Will anyone else be required to attend; if contended facts emerge will witnesses be needed?

— Decide the best time to convene the interview.

- **Dos and Don'ts**
  - Do not get involved in arguments.
  - Avoid physical contact.
  - Don't use the opportunity to harangue the employee: state the complaint as briefly and concisely as possible.
  - Don't raise your voice or become abusive, and observe the normal social courtesies.
  - Do not try to humiliate or make personal remarks.
  - Avoid sarcasm, particularly with younger employees.
  - Restrict your body movement whilst speaking and don't fiddle around with objects on the desk.
  - Try to avoid tension in the body posture, facial expression and in your voice.
  - Maintain eye contact with the employee.
  - Don't joke or smile extravagantly. Seriousness of purpose should be registered throughout.

- **Procedure**
  - Tell the employee what the substance of the complaint is.
  - Show the employee any data to emphasise the point and explain it to him.
  - Ask the employee if there is any reason or mitigating circumstance that ought to be considered: encourage the employee to talk.
  - Consider the reasons/explanation put forward by the employee. Evaluate:
    - (a) Is the employee entirely at fault or was someone else responsible? Was it an organisational failure?
    - (b) If it was the employee's fault, are there any personal or other mitigating circumstances to take into account?
    - (c) Are the explanations just excuses?

- — Ask the employee what he or she intends to do to remedy the situation.

- — Search jointly for a solution that will address the problem and allow the employee to make the necessary improvements.

- — Summarise the interview and make sure the employee is told that the interview must be treated as an informal warning and what steps will be taken next if improvements in performance or conduct are not forthcoming. Specify any time limits agreed for performance or conduct to be reviewed.

- — Make a note of the proceedings in a diary or on a file.

● **Monitoring**

If time limits are agreed, ensure that you reinterview when that time limit has been reached. If satisfactory progress has been made let the employee know. If progress is unsatisfactory you must take formal action as specified by the company disciplinary procedure. See Chapter 5 on "Making it Formal".

5   Making it Formal

If all the efforts of the manager have failed at the informal stages without the necessary improvement being made then it is time to initiate a first level formal written warning and go through the procedure until it is finally exhausted. Sometimes more serious forms of misconduct may justify an immediate written warning. Outlined below is a checklist of considerations to be taken into account before taking steps to give a formal written warning.

Checklist: When to take Formal Disciplinary Action

- Has any period of time for improvement been fully completed without the employee achieving the required standards with regard to their conduct or job performance?

- Has the same or similar incident of minor misconduct, ie rudeness, inattention to work, etc, occurred again?

- Has the incident occurred within a reasonable period of time after the informal warning? (Anything longer than six months would not be reasonable.)

- Is the act of misconduct rather more serious than that which normally merits an informal warning?

- Is the act of misconduct a breach of the written company rules for which a formal written warning is prescribed?

  If the answer to any one of these questions is yes, then a formal warning should be given.

Where to Find the Procedures

Many organisations have written disciplinary procedures that have been agreed with the recognised trade union (if appropriate) and are incorporated into each individual employee's contract of employment by either being physically written into the terms and conditions statement or into an incorporated document such as a company handbook, union agreement, etc. This has the distinct advantage that both parties know precisely what steps will be taken.

Why Keep to the Procedure?

If there is a procedure laid down then you must follow it. Every manager must read thoroughly and understand exactly how the disciplinary procedure works. Even slight failures to follow the laid down procedure can cause problems with trade union officials, who will seize on any procedural irregularity to defend their members. Furthermore, if the matter ultimately goes to an industrial tribunal the decision may go against the employer because of the oversight. There may be circumstances where failing to follow slavishly the procedure can be justified:

(a) where the procedure actually allows stages to be jumped for specific offences or at management discretion;

(b) by circumstances where in the disciplinary interview employees indicate that they are clearly set on going their own way and will not co-operate or will not accept that they have done anything wrong.

Many other organisations have no written procedures at all to guide managers in coping with disciplinary problems and neither are there any written rules or regulations setting out the standards of conduct required, so it may be useful to look at an example procedure that is based on the ACAS Code of Practice but has been adapted to a small non-unionised company. A very different kind of procedure will be required for a company where, say, there are many branch offices or shops or where there is a recognised trade union that will be involved in the disciplinary process.

Whatever the type of procedure adopted there are certain universal features and points to look out for when operating them.

Example Disciplinary Procedure for Small Non-unionised Companies

Objective

The purpose of the company's disciplinary procedure is to ensure the safe and effective operation of the business and the fair treatment of individual employees.

Procedures

1. Informal Warnings

Minor breaches of company discipline, misconduct, failure to maintain job performance standards, poor timekeeping, etc, will result in an oral warning given by your immediate superior. A note of this warning will be made in daybook/ clockcard/personnel record card, etc.

It is unlikely that any other further action will be necessary as in most cases an oral warning will quickly resolve most difficulties.

Where there is a more serious breach of company discipline or misconduct or an employee fails to improve and maintain that improvement in relation to conduct or job performance formal disciplinary action will be taken.

2. Formal Warnings

- A disciplinary interview conducted by .... will be held. Employees may be accompanied by another employee of the company if they so wish.

- Employees will be informed of the nature of the complaint and such evidence as may exist. Employees may present their explanation of the matter.

- If it is decided that disciplinary action should be taken the employee will be told of the decision and later given a letter in confirmation.

- The employee will be told, and the written confirmation will state:

  (a) details of the misconduct, poor performance or other matter that has occasioned the warning;

  (b) details of the necessary action to remedy the situation, outlining precisely what standard is expected and any period of review, extra training, etc, decided on;

  (c) that any further misconduct, or expiry of the review period without significant and sustained improvement, will result in:

    (i) dismissal with appropriate contractual notice, or
    (ii) a further disciplinary interview and confirmed final warning which, if unheeded, will result in dismissal with the appropriate notice.

- The final decision to dismiss can only be taken by .... after he or she has satisfied himself or herself with regard to the facts of the case; whether or not there are any mitigating circumstances, and interviewing the employee concerned.

- Some alternatives short of dismissal may be considered. They are as follows:

  (a) suspension without pay up to a maximum of seven days;

  (b) demotion and associated loss of pay to a more suitable job, if available;

  (c) transfer to other premises, department, etc.

3. Dismissal Without Warnings

In rare circumstances the employee will be summarily dismissed without notice if it is established, after investigation and hearing the employee's version of the matter, that there has been an act of gross misconduct, major breach of duty or conduct that brings the company into disrepute. In particular this includes:

insubordination;

serious breach of safety rules potentially involving loss of life or limb;

theft or fraud;

breach of clocking rules;

being under the influence of drink or drugs during working hours;

flagrant failure to follow company documentary procedures or regulations;

breach of duty regarding non-disclosure of confidential information;

deliberate damage to company property or that of other employees;

disorderly or indecent conduct, fighting on company premises of threatening physical violence;

acts of incitement or actual acts of discrimination on the grounds of sex, race, religion, colour or ethnic origin.

4. Suspension

At any stage of the disciplinary procedure the employee may be suspended with pay whilst the circumstances of any complaint are being investigated.

5. Appeals

At any stage of the disciplinary procedure the employee may appeal to .... either orally or in writing against any disciplinary action taken providing the appeal is made within 48 hours of that action being taken.

Key Aspects of Operating the Procedure

1. Object of the Procedure

The employer who drafted the procedure outlined above is to be congratulated because he or she avoided calling the procedure a "dismissal" procedure! The objective is clearly stated in the opening paragraph and indicates the spirit and intention of the procedure — it is remedial; all employees have access to it (sometimes employers do have different procedures for different groups of workers) and its aim is to rehabilitate. Managers have a clear responsibility to operate disciplinary procedures in this manner. Disciplinary procedures should not be seen merely as a way to get rid of people whilst appearing to go through the motions of a fair dismissal.

Now, keeping to some of the highly developed (long-winded) procedures can be infuriating to a manager who knows he or she has a "bad one" and wants to get rid of that employee quickly. However, there is nothing more unpleasant than doing it in a hurry and then having a tribunal decision awarded against you, and the information filtering back to other employees in the company in a highly distorted way. "Softly, softly . . ." is the best approach.

2. Informal Warnings, Reprimands

The section on informal warnings makes no mention of an interview but this is by far the best way to operate the procedure at every stage. (A closer look at informal procedures is contained in the Chapter beginning on page 31.)

It is not just a pious hope that in most cases there will be no need to go further than this informal level. Most employees only require to be spoken to in a constructive, clear way and they will try to put matters right. If the employee does not, for whatever reason, there is a provision in the procedure to give formal written warnings. Most procedures allow for this informal stage to be left out in a more serious case of misconduct.

Many companies operate a totting-up system whereby lateness and absence warnings are totted-up and counted together, ie six informal warnings in three months for either reason results in a formal written warning. Special care must be taken when operating such a procedure because it soon becomes apparent that some employees have become experts at working the system, ie never getting the sixth informal warning and relying on the six months' life span of the warning to write off old offences (some written procedures only give a three month life span for informal warnings). Some appallingly bad attendance records are fuelled by such disciplinary procedures and require a little ingenuity on the part of the manager to make disciplinary action effective (see Chapter 6 on Putting it into Practice). Without such a totting-up system, great care should be exercised to ensure that it is only repeats of the same offence that are dealt with progressively by disciplinary action. An informal warning for lateness cannot be followed in the first instance with a written warning for absence and later, a final warning for poor workmanship.

3. How to Give a Written Warning

It is important to note that even at the formal stages great priority is given to holding a disciplinary interview. There should be no attempt at avoiding a "face to face" session with the employee by just jotting off a few lines of complaint and warning, popping it in the post box or leaving it in a sealed envelope on the employee's desk or in a pay packet. Tribunals utterly deplore this kind of approach and quite rightly so. It is also an ineffective method of getting commitment from employees to change their ways. Additionally, employees have no chance to state their case, give details of any mitigating circumstances and correct any inaccuracies in the facts that have told against them. It is most embarrassing to be forced to withdraw warnings that cannot be substantiated and in some circumstances it could give grounds for the employee to claim constructive dismissal.

4. The Right to be Accompanied at the Interview

Even if the procedure does not state that the employee may be accompanied at the interview it is always a good idea to ask if they would like someone else to be present (see section on Formal Disciplinary Interview, page 65).

5. Prior Indication

Employees should be given some indication of the purpose of the meeting before they go into it. This is good practice because they will have a chance to consider what is being alleged against them and sort out what they are going to say in their own defence. It may well be that they will choose to get some advice from their union, solicitor or citizens advice bureau.

(No union official may attend such a meeting without agreement of the parties unless the union is recognised. Similarly, solicitors do not have a right to attend though very often employers agree to such a move when they know their case is strong so that justice can be seen to be done. In principle it is not a good idea to involve non-company personnel in such an interview.)

6. When The Letter Should Be Given

The main ground rules for disciplinary meetings have already been discussed on page 35 and will be dealt with again in the next section. The main difference now that we have entered the formal part of the procedure is that a formal written document results, a copy of which is given to the employee after the disciplinary interview. Don't be tempted to write it up complete with signature and hand it to the employee at the beginning or at the end of the interview. This would indicate a very cynical approach which would show that you were just going through the motions. Anything the employee might say on his or her own behalf would not have been taken into account.

There is no need for the employee to sign the written warning, particularly if a disciplinary interview takes place before it is issued, because it is simply an accurate confirmation of what was said.

So far as accepting warnings is concerned, the employee is in a difficult position: the only effective way of protesting against a warning is to appeal to a company director or follow whatever procedure is specified to accomplish an appeal against disciplinary action. If that fails, then the employee's only recourse is to leave employment and claim constructive dismissal on the basis that the warning was completely contrived in order to get rid of him or her. Ripping up the warning will have no effect and the employer may consider it served if the contents are read formally to the employee and a copy is placed in the individual's personnel file.

7. Procedural Flexibility

The example procedure given has a great deal of flexibility built into it, which is ideal for a small company. It is not realistic to expect a lengthy procedure going to three written warnings before a final written warning is reached from a small company where employees are well known and disharmony can be deeply destructive. They do not have the same resources as larger organisations and all employees must pull their weight. In larger companies an employee may have more than one manager during the course of a year and extensive written procedures are the only way to keep tabs on things. These several levels of formal written warnings are usually a response to the size of the organisation and the degree of unionisation.

All the law requires is that a fair procedure is used. Although the ACAS Code of Practice (see page 7) sets out guidelines, there are many ways a disciplinary procedure can be fashioned without following it in every detail, yet still remain a fair procedure. In the example at the beginning of this chapter the option is given either to have a final written warning or a first written warning depending on the nature of the misconduct and other mitigating circumstances, such as previous long unblemished service, personal circumstances, etc, that may be taken into account.

8. Life Span of Warnings

In the example procedure there is no life span laid down for these warnings and there is a good reason for this. If a situation arose where a senior manager was found to have worked in competition with the company it would normally justify his or her immediate dismissal. If, however, he or she had important skills and was prepared to agree that he or she would not continue such a practice, a final written warning specifying that dismissal would follow any further disloyalty might well be given. It would be essential to give a formal warning to show that the conduct was not approved or condoned and it would be nonsense for such a warning only to have a six month life span.

Simply, it depends on the nature of the offence, the seniority of the employee and what is considered reasonable in the circumstances. In general, warnings for minor offences can only be valid for a maximum of six months whilst more serious offences that result in final warnings may remain in force for 12 months or more. Do not try to use old expired warnings to build a case against an employee nor incidents for which no warning was given at the time.

9. Final Warning and Dismissal

Once again, if there has been no improvement or the same misconduct is committed again, the next stage in the procedure is initiated. If a first warning had been given, then another interview will confirm a final warning. If the last warning was a final one that threatened dismissal, then the interview will revolve around the possibility of finding some lesser penalty than dismissal (in most cases this will not be possible).

Any final decision to dismiss is usually reserved for senior managers or directors who, if they have not been involved up to now, must familiarise themselves with the case and interview the employee. If a tribunal action results they most certainly will be required to give evidence and dismissal by remote control is not very convincing even if they were acting on reports of other managers.

Appeals

It is quite usual for disciplinary procedures to contain an appeals procedure so that if employees are dissatisfied and do not believe they have received a fair hearing, they should be told or reminded of the existence of this procedure, and that it can be used at any stage when warnings are given. In effect, it is a safety valve to check that things have been done properly and to ensure that bias is eliminated.

This appeals provision is quite separate from the normal grievance procedure which employees use when they want to complain about always being put on a job they don't like, or having to work with a particular person, or when they feel that refusal of holiday leave or their grading is unfair.

Example Grievance Procedure for Small Non-unionised Companies

If an employee wishes to discuss a grievance or raise a query arising from his or her employment, the matter should be raised with the immediate manager. If a satisfactory solution is not reached in three working days the employee can raise the matter with a director of the company. This can be done either orally or in writing.

After consultation, the director will give his or her decision within five working days. There are no further levels of appeal. This procedure applies to both individual and collective grievances.

Disciplinary appeals procedures, on the other hand, usually only have one level and it is directed to the top of the management structure. Sometimes there is provision for the matter to go to arbitration. This enables the decision to be reviewed by someone with the authority to put it right promptly if it was a bad decision.

Even in small companies where the employer is effectively involved in all levels of discipline, including the decision to dismiss, an appeals procedure will allow a review at a more composed and less harassed time. Ideally, the employee should be interviewed by the person hearing the appeal. There is no need for the decision to be given there and then; a letter explaining the reasons for the rejection (or acceptance) later would be quite permissible. The person hearing the appeal may well think it sensible to do his or her own checking if the employee has thrown up anything interesting

Some General Points

1.   A question often asked is how soon after a final warning can we dismiss?

Well, if the matter revolves around a specific act of misconduct, ie insubordination to a supervisor or smoking in a non-smoking area, the employee can be dismissed the next time the offence is repeated. If it is the type of offence for which patterns emerge over time, ie lateness, poor attendance, etc, then it is safer to give a period of review and when that period expires decide whether or not the required standard has been met. If not, then dismissal will result.

2.   Another question frequently posed is "we told him that

we would give him three months to improve, he'll never make it so can we let him go now?''

This may be quite a valid assessment of a sales representative's abilities but by not giving the whole of the period stated you may give good grounds for an unfair dismissal claim. After all, he may get all the necessary orders to reach his targets in the last month of the review period. Be on the safe side and give the benefit of the full review period. If some other more serious incident happens in the meantime or there is some clear evidence that the employee is sitting at home doing nothing, there will be sufficient grounds to bring forward the dismissal.

3. "How long should a review period last for?"

From tribunal case law, such factors as length of service and nature of the job are the main determining factors to be balanced against the need for the company to replace with a competent or more reliable employee. Certainly nothing can be achieved by a period of less than one week; two weeks or a month would be better. A long service employee could expect three to six months as a reasonable review period.

4. Surely, say some employers, we don't have to go through these procedures if the employee doesn't have two years' service?

There are various factors to look at before you can provide an answer to that question. First, are you sure that the employee hasn't got two years' service? Count the total service accurately; if they were dismissed with pay in lieu of notice they can still add on the statutory notice requirement (one week) to their total length of service even though they did not work it. Consequently, just under two years' actual service may be enough to claim unfair dismissal at a tribunal.

Second, is your disciplinary procedure a part of the contract of employment? If it has been incorporated, then by failing to follow it you are in breach of contract and have wrongfully dismissed the employee. Although he or she cannot take the fairness of the dismissal to the industrial tribunal a claim can be made to a county court alleging breach of contract. The likely damages will be determined for a period that would represent the time it would take to go through the disciplinary procedure and the appropriate period of notice. The best reason for using the disciplinary procedure with all staff regardless of service is that it is good personnel practice and should not take an impossibly long time if action is promptly initiated by the first line manager.

Gross Misconduct

Finally, the example procedure shows that certain acts will be classified as gross misconduct and details the action which will be taken to deal with such problems.

In most organisations serious acts of misconduct are dealt with by senior management although the immediate manager is often involved when the matter is discovered. Often it is how the manager initially handles the situation that will either help or hinder the senior manager when he or she comes to deal with the problem.

How do you recognise gross misconduct and what steps should the manager take? Actions that are considered to be gross misconduct can vary between organisations and where there are written rules these offences are often listed and classified. Even without specific rules certain conduct is almost universally treated as gross misconduct — theft, fraud, physical violence, insubordination, refusal to carry out reasonable orders, etc. These are, in fact, actions that go to the root of the contract and will destroy it. An employer cannot trust anyone who is a thief or who is likely to become violent or insubordinate.

The crucial aspect is: has the conduct destroyed the relationship between the employer and employee? There may be circumstances in which the relationship can still survive and continue in spite of obvious acts of gross misconduct on the employee's part.

Many employers continue to employ people who they know are thieves because they feel that once the employee has been "fingered" he or she won't do it again. Alternatively, if employees only took waste materials of little value the employer may prefer to retain their services rather than penalise them disproportionately. Perhaps their jobs can be rearranged so that they won't handle cash any more and so temptation won't arise.

In other words, there is a whole range of responses open to an employer so that he or she need not necessarily seize the opportunity to dismiss the erring employee. One employer decided that because he had employed the employee's whole family he did not want to sour these relationships by dismissing the employee who had been caught red-handed.

Another was affected by his employee's long unblemished service record which to him weighed more heavily than the £300 stolen to pay a debt. In other circumstances, dismissal has been eschewed when the employee promptly promised to pay the missing sums of money.

Similar considerations apply to most acts of gross misconduct — they can be mitigated by the circumstances and the employer does not dismiss. This has always been the case and the laws of unfair dismissal reflect this custom and practice.

The employer will always have a good reason to dismiss, without notice, any employee whom he can show fought, stole, etc, but will also have to show that the decision was reasonable given all the surrounding circumstances, including how the matter was investigated and was put to the employee to explain. Even the reliance on a written rule stating that acts of theft will result in immediate dismissal will not ensure that the employee's dismissal is automatically fair.

An industrial tribunal looks at all these circumstances including consistency in enforcing such rules, the degree to which conduct in condoned, etc. The example procedure reflects this requirement. It provides for investigation, hearing the employee's version of the matter at an interview and the proper consideration of anything that might show the employee in a better light, or perhaps excuse what has been done, before a decision to dismiss is made.

Suspension During Investigation

It is often necessary to suspend an employee from work whilst an investigation is carried out. Having the employee off the premises usually ensures that bits of information trickle in that wouldn't normally do so and people won't stand around in groups waiting for the next bit of fun to break out. If the employee is told to return the next day or is subsequently instructed to return by letter or telephone after completion of the investigation, tempers have cooled and a more constructive approach can be adopted.

Does the employee have to receive pay whilst he is suspended? Sometimes it is agreed at the time of the incident that the pay will not be given but if, subsequently, the allegation is shown to be without foundation backpay will be given. (Written procedures often have this provision.) Alternatively, the employee's written terms of employment will specify that pay is or is not given during suspension.

In law, there is no general right to stop the employee from working when he or she is willing and able, and the employer must pay during that period of suspension unless the contract of employment contains the right to withhold payment. As a general rule it is better to pay an employee who is suspended when disciplinary matters are being investigated because withdrawal of pay is already starting to punish him or her before any of the facts have been determined and so presupposes "guilt".

Suspension can also be used in a penalising way, very often as an alternative to dismissal. Sometimes, disciplinary procedures provide for a scale of short suspensions depending on the offence and its frequency. Usually the suspensions last for two or three days and are intended as a short sharp shock. Over-long periods of unpaid suspension are undesirable on two counts. It is a penalty that is inequitable: it won't affect some employees as greatly as those with dependants who have greater financial responsibilities; additionally, it may "reward" absence from work or lateness with yet more time off work. Similarly, the practice of sending home employees who turn up impossibly late for work is not an effective control method if used too frequently.

Making the Situation Tidy

For the manager, who will not be involved in the ultimate decision, the most important contribution he or she can make is to ensure that the situation is tidy: provide the senior manager with a detailed report of the circumstances and assist with the investigation. In most cases a "tidy" situation means that the employee is suspended until an investigation can be completed and the employee is called back to work later to be interviewed, before a decision is made about continued employment. In incidents where physical violence is used the supervisor will have to get the people concerned off the company premises as quickly as possible. It should be made clear to them that they are suspended, not dismissed. This can de-escalate the situation quite quickly. If the contestants are affected by alcohol it is even more important not to enter into long discussions but to clear them off the premises until they have sobered up. If any employee refuses to leave, a phone call to the police can usually provide the solution.

The manager should try to take accurate statements from those who witnessed the incident. Simply get them to relate, step by step in their own words, what they saw and heard. Make sure that sufficient detail is put in, state the time of the incident, the date, who else was there, etc, and set it all out in a written statement. Put in a little diagram of where people were standing if this will help the reader's understanding. Then pin the statements to a report outlining all facts in chronological order. An example of such a report follows on the next page.

The use of a written report completed soon after the incident is extremely helpful later when memories have dimmed. If such an incident results in dismissal and tribunal action, it is always several months before evidence is given and references to such a document can prod the memory into action.

To: John Brown, General Manager
From: Peter Davy, Engineering Section Manager

When I returned to the Engineering Department after
lunch at 1.30 pm today I was met by Robert Henry who
told me that there was a fight in the stores between Jim
Smith and Len Pearce (both fitters grade II). When I
reached the store the two men had been restrained by
other employees but both were very upset and angry.
Pearce went to the stores and I had Smith brought over
to my office.

Smith said that the argument was over a lost wrench
that was owned by Pearce who had accused him of
stealing it. Pearce had thrown a spanner at him and said:
"You might as well have that bastard as well". Smith
added that the spanner slid along the bench and
dropped at his feet. It never touched him. Pearce started
pushing Smith, threatening to thump him and blows
started to be thrown. They were restrained by other
employees shortly after. Smith had bad grazes around
the eyes and facial bruising but otherwise he was not
seriously hurt. I told him that he was suspended until
tomorrow at 10.00 am, when he should report to the
General Manager's office for a disciplinary meeting.

Next, I spoke to Pearce whose account was almost
identical. He insisted he had not thrown the spanner at
Smith, merely pushed it along the bench in disgust and
it fell off the bench. Pearce was similarly suspended until
10.00 am the next day. I went back to speak to the other
employees to see who else had seen what happened. I
enclose the statement of Richard Turney.

Relevant Background Information
Both men have been involved in disagreements that
have resulted in informal warnings for indiscipline and
two months ago they were both given a strong talking to
and as a transfer was impossible their work areas was
separated.

L. Pearce Engaged 4.10.88 No previous written warnings
J. Smith   Engaged 18.5.90 No previous written warnings

Action Other Than Dismissal

The example procedure makes it necessary to consider any other action that might be possible to penalise the employee rather than taking the ultimate step of dismissal. There may be quite a variety of sanctions that can be applied; generally they include demotion, transfer, loss of wages or other benefits.

Demotion

In most cases unilateral demotion of an employee would be considered a major breach of contract unless it is justified as a penultimate stage in the disciplinary procedure, ie after taking the normal steps to warn the employee (and give such training and assistance as necessary if the issue is job performance). This is not always an acceptable solution and the employee may prefer to be dismissed rather than return to the tools amongst employees whom he or she previously controlled. Sometimes it is sensible to arrange a transfer to another department or arrange another job title and a different seating arrangement or change of office so that the demotion can be seen by others as a change of responsibility, not as a stark demotion.

One thing should also be considered: when will the punishment end? Will the employee never again be considered for promotion or after, say, a year of good behaviour will the individual be able to reapply for a responsible job? Such conditions should be spelt out to the employee.

Transfers

Transfers are often considered quite early in the disciplinary procedure, especially where the problems relate to personality clashes or failure to cope with particular types of work. Transfer can also be used as an alternative to dismissal where it may involve moving to a less pleasant job, less opportunity to earn productivity bonuses or reduction of basic wage rate, etc. Removal from friends and associates is all part of the punitive effect.

Similarly, some thought should be given to when the

employee will be "brought in from the cold" and be able to resume the previous job.

Termination of Employment

Alternative action other than dismissal is not always possible, especially in smaller concerns, and dismissal is then the only feasible option. The example procedure defines the circumstances in which notice is given or not given to end the contract of employment. If the warning procedure has been completed then notice must be given.

It is important to note that notice should not run concurrently with a review period, ie "you are given four weeks' notice of dismissal and during this time you must improve your attendance and timekeeping. If you reach an acceptable standard your notice of dismissal will be withdrawn". Notice of dismissal cannot be withdrawn unilaterally and the employee may not accept the withdrawal and leave anyway — claiming unfair dismissal. Giving notice of dismissal under the guise of a warning is not a fair procedure — the warning procedure has to be completed before notice is given, consequently there is quite a possibility that a tribunal would find such a dismissal unfair.

The Formal Disciplinary Interview

Once the informal level has been passed, more senior managers usually become involved in the disciplinary action although the first line manager still has a role to play. It is a good idea to discuss the problems with a departmental manager even if your company procedure allows the immediate manager to give the first written warning. Often the procedure requires the personnel department to be involved once the formal stage is reached; some even require the personnel officer to conduct the interview and give the warning.

Clearly procedures have tremendous variety but in all of them the immediate manager will greatly assist if he or she prepares a simple written report outlining the problems and the action taken so far. If it is a serious matter that is going straight into the formal procedure, with no previous informal action having been taken, the report will outline the incident and how the situation was "tidied up". If the warning has been given then the manager usually has the responsibility of monitoring progress. Therefore, involvement in the interview is important just so that he or she knows what the position is.

The formal disciplinary interview itself will not vary greatly from the informal disciplinary interview. The aims and ways of going about it remain the same but there are features and considerations which come out more strongly at this level. (See Figure 3 at the end of this chapter.)

Calling the Meeting

When the employee is called to the meeting, sometimes this is done by letter. A clear outline should be given of what allegations or complaints are to be faced. The date and venue should be given as should details of who will be in attendance.

If it is a very serious matter that is likely to end in dismissal, there is no harm in pointing this out, eg dismissal is to be considered unless the employee is able to provide an adequate explanation of the situation or mitigating circumstances.

It is not unknown for employees to resign or not turn up to such an interview because they know they have no adequate explanation or mitigating factors to help them.

If the employee does not turn up, an explanation for the non-attendance should be sought, perhaps a new date set, and the warning given that if he or she does not turn up again (without adequate reason) dismissal will be effected.

Minutes

It is sensible for the person conducting the interview to take notes of the conversation. This is particularly important if it is an issue involving gross misconduct. Include any answers or explanations that the employee might give. These notes will form the basis of the written warning.

Sometimes the manager may feel that it is necessary to take a tape recording of the situation. Ideally, this should not be done without the employee knowing that the interview is going down on tape. From the point of unfair dismissal actions it is very rare for tribunals to admit recordings as evidence and they will usually only do so when it was known by all the participants at the time that a tape-recording was being made.

Witnesses to the Interview

Does there have to be a witness present? It is not essential but a secretary taking notes is very useful. The employee may wish to be accompanied by a colleague or a recognised union representative and in that case the presence of someone else on the management team would be sensible.

Witnesses

At the formal stages it is more likely that witnesses will have to be introduced into the meeting because more serious disciplinary incidents are involved. It is sufficient to relate precisely to the employee what has been discovered about the incident and that there are witnesses to support this view. If the employee does not challenge this view and accepts that these are essentially the true facts of the situation, there is no need to involve witnesses. If a challenge is made to any of the facts it is essential that witnesses are brought to the meeting and asked to repeat again their previous statements. They may have given signed statements but if the recalcitrant employee is adamant and his or her version of the facts is feasible then he or she must have the chance to question those who have made allegations against him or her. Additionally, this helps management, because unless you see both employees together you have little opportunity to assess who really is telling the truth.

This should not be an opportunity for an argument or confrontation between the two people involved. Keep the proceedings to recounting what the witness saw and answering questions from the accused employee.

Sometimes the allegations come from customers or

business associates who would not be prepared to attend. In this case some form of written statement will have to suffice. The employee should be shown a copy of any such statement. If the employee challenges the accuracy of the allegation then the employer must tactfully put the explanation to the customer or business associate and see what reply is given. In the end the employer must decide whom to believe.

Investigation

Very often managers are faced with two completely different tales, quite persuasively put to them; so what happens then?

There may be no conclusive evidence one way or the other. However, the impression can be formed that one set of events is more likely to be true that another. Knowing the recalcitrant employee, the veracity of the witness, etc, in these circumstances the employer must be able to show that he or she carried out all the investigation that could reasonably be expected. Don't be thrown by these events. Adjourn the proceedings to check out the stories and decide if other relevant investigations could be made to get corroboration for one side or the other. (This situation can happen quite frequently if disciplinary action has been initiated without proper investigation beforehand and the adjournment will help to repair the situation without any loss of face.) When investigations are complete the interviewing manager must decide which version of the facts is to be believed and why; not which version of the facts has been proved beyond all reasonable doubt. It is not a High Court standard of proof you are looking for.

An employer cannot investigate too thoroughly: in fact the investigation is good insurance. If, after the dismissal, it turns out that new evidence shows that the employee was not to blame or the court does not convict for theft, etc, it will not rebound on to the employer's head at an industrial tribunal if the investigation was rigorous. It may seem very unfair that the person has been penalised for something that could not be proven or that he or she did not do. However, the employer's defence will be that "at the time the decision was made, after extensive investigation, I had reasonable grounds to believe that the employee was responsible". All things being equal, this should be sufficient defence (see page 94 for further discussion of dismissal for theft).

If the investigation supports the employee's story or puts the allegations in too much doubt then quash the proceedings immediately; you will not lose face — it is the right thing to do.

Shop Stewards

Another problem of which managers must be aware is that any formal disciplinary action taken against a recognised shop steward ought to be delayed until the ACAS Code of Practice recommendations can be followed, ie the matter should be discussed with the convenor or the full-time union official.

This recognises the industrial relations dimension of the problem and should not be seen as an attempt to treat them differently or apply different standards of behaviour or job performance. Disciplinary action taken against recognised shop stewards is often seen as an attack on the union and frequently results in industrial action being taken in their support. It is sensible to clear the path before action is taken.

How to Give a Written Warning

The interview that precedes the confirmed written warning will follow the same overall pattern of the informal disciplinary interview:

- make sure that the setting is comfortable and that adequate seating is available. Interruptions by telephone should be prevented and a "do not disturb" sign on the door will also help. Keep the approach formal but friendly. Make sure that noise levels are not excessive;

- do not lose your temper or raise your voice and observe all the usual social courtesies. See page 34 for other useful hints;

69

- ask the employee if he or she wishes any colleague or the recognised trade union representative to accompany him or her;

- since he or she has already been informed of the purpose of the meeting it would be quite permissible to launch straight in and ask for an explanation but a better tactic when dealing with non-gross misconduct issues is to summarise the steps that have been taken to date to discuss, assist and warn the employee about the conduct or job performance, asking at each point whether he or she agrees that this has happened. If standards are still unacceptable, show the documentary evidence, if any, and ask what he or she makes of it. Ask whether he or she thinks the performance has improved and has he or she really tried to make an effort. Try to get the two-way conversation going from the outset. Ask if there is any explanation for the failure to improve. Search for possible reasons and if some personal problems seem to be at the back of it consider if there is any action that the company can take to assist (it may not have been done very effectively at the informal stage or subsequent problems may have occurred). Explain to the employee that, although feeling sympathetic to any personal difficulties, the warning procedure will continue and eventually dismissal is likely to result.

- Evaluate any reasons/excuses given by the employee;

- once again, specify time limits for improvement and indicate that the improvement must be consistently maintained. Set clear standards of job performance to be attained;

- explain that the warning is a first (or second formal or final) written warning and written confirmation will be given later, based on the notes of the meeting;

- make it clear what the next step in the procedure will be if standards are not met or the incident of misconduct occurs again;

- tell the employee that if he or she is dissatisfied about the disciplinary action taken, an appeal can be made. Specify what the appeal procedure is.

Checklist: Formal Disciplinary Interview

Preliminary Steps

- Make sure you have all the relevant facts available including any appropriate documents.

- Define precisely what the complaint is, ie is it a breach of the company's till procedures or an allegation of taking money from the till? (the former might be the better approach if hard evidence of theft is hard to find).

- Consider what excuses might be offered and check them out beforehand.

- Confirm by letter the purpose of the disciplinary meeting or explain verbally to the employee beforehand what it is about. If it is a complex issue involving documentation, it is useful to give copies in advance or you may have to adjourn the meeting to allow the employee to study this.

- Make notes of the matters you intend to raise.

- Arrange a witness of the proceedings to be present. It is useful if notes can be taken.

- Inform the employee of his or her right to be accompanied by a colleague or recognised trade union representative.

- Should witnesses to the incidents be required, can you round them up at short notice to attend the meeting?

- If the employee to be disciplined is a recognised shop steward, has the convenor or full-time official been consulted before action is taken?

Procedure

- Recap on previous disciplinary action taken for the offence or failure to meet standards and restate the problem. Do not jump to conclusions and start thinking of the penalties; satisfy yourself that the employee is at fault.

- Ask whether there is any explanation to account for the failure to improve or for the recurrence of the misconduct. Evaluate the reasons given:

- — Is the employee entirely at fault or was someone else responsible? Was it an organisational failure outside the employee's control?
- — Are there any personal or other mitigating circumstances to be taken into account?
- — Are the explanations just excuses? If so make it clear you do not accept them.

● If the employee has provided an adequate explanation or there is no real evidence to support the allegation, do not be afraid to quash the proceedings then and there.

● If evidence is a little thin on the ground but there is some merit in the allegation, reopen the investigation after adjourning the meeting. Always check out contended facts again.

● Decide on the balance of probabilities what version of the facts is true.

● Tell the employee your decision and then consider with the employee:
  - — what action can be taken to help solve the problem, ie retraining, transfer to a different department;
  - — what penalty should be given, eg first written warning or, if the matter is serious, a final written warning (if your company procedure allows this flexibility);
  - — clear targets or performance standards, or specify what is expected of the employee;
  - — decide on a review period, if appropriate, when the matter will be assessed;
  - — indicate what the next stage in the procedure is if the assessment is unfavourable or the act of misconduct is committed again (follow what is specified in your company procedure);

● Explain the appeals procedure if the employee is unhappy about the disciplinary action.

● Make sure a letter is given/sent to the employee outlining the substance of the interview.

Final Written Warnings and Dismissal

When coming to the end of the disciplinary procedure, a final warning must be given stating unequivocally that a repeat of the misconduct or failure to improve after a reasonable period will result in dismissal, with appropriate notice being given. Do not water it down, ie "may be dismissed". Such a warning must be confirmed in writing to the employee after the disciplinary meeting. When the situation is reviewed again and there has been no improvement or there has been a repeat of the misconduct, another interview must be convened to take action to dismiss the employee. Never dismiss by letter, always try to see the employee first.

Checklist Part 1: Dismissal After Warning

- Is dismissal being effected at the expiry of the review period and has performance or conduct been unsatisfactory?

- Is it a repeat of an act of misconduct for which a final warning has been previously given? If so, is it a reasonable period of time since the warning was given, considering the nature of the offence and any lifetime limit to the warning?

- Are there any mitigating circumstances to consider?

- Is an other penalty short of dismissal feasible?

- Decide whether you require notice to be worked.

- Inform the employee at the interview of the appeal procedure.

- Confirm dismissal, notice, outstanding pay and other termination instructions in a letter.

- If written reasons for dismissal are requested by the employee or required by your procedure, write giving full details of the reason for dismissal, the stages of warning gone through and enclose copies of previous written warnings.

Checklist Part 2: Dismissal for Gross Misconduct

● Has the employee been brought back from suspension for a disciplinary interview?

● Are you satisfied that on reasonable grounds, after full investigation, the employee was at fault and to blame? Did the employee know that breach of the rule or particular act of misconduct would be treated as gross misconduct? Ignorance is no defence if he or she might reasonably have been expected to know.

● Has the employee had the opportunity to state his or her case?

● Consistency: has dismissal always been the penalty attached to the breach of the rules or the act of gross misconduct, or have there been different solutions in the past? If so, why was there a departure from the normal penalty on previous occasions? If the circumstances are the same now, you will also have to consider a similar lesser penalty.

● Are there any mitigating circumstances that ought to be taken into consideration?

● Is there any lesser penalty that can be used in this situation?

Note

Once it has been decided that an employee will be dismissed for gross misconduct, notice should not be given except in very rare circumstances. There is no liability to give pay in lieu of notice though some employers do so as an *ex gratia* payment. Additionally, all payments earned up to the date of dismissal should be paid including accrued holiday pay, unless there is any contractual term that allows accrued holiday payments not to be paid.

Written Reasons

Written reasons must be provided within 14 days of the employee's oral or written request, detailing exactly the reasons for dismissal, providing the employee has at least 2 years service. It would, though, be good personnel practice to comply with such a request regardless of the length of service.

Some company disciplinary procedures require reasons to be given in writing automatically even if the employee does not make the request. The statement must be in writing (it is sensible to send it by recorded delivery) and there must be sufficiently detailed information contained in it to make the situation clear to any interested party. If previous correspondence exists, ie warning letters, dismissal letters, etc, it is a good idea to attach them as well.

It is a most important document because it is admissible in any unfair dismissal hearing, so take care in its drafting. An example of such a letter follows on the next page.

Example: Written Reasons for Dismissal

Dear Mr Dodds

Further to your request for written reasons for dismissal we would confirm that the reason was your lack of capability to perform your job reliably because of your addiction to alcohol.

As you are aware, the situation has been the subject of several meetings over the past eighteen months. We enclose the letters sent to you after each meeting. The matter came to our attention because your attendance and timekeeping had begun to deteriorate very badly. During the meeting your underlying drink problem was discussed and, as a result of a visit to the company doctor, you were given one month's leave to take remedial treatment.

When you returned to work we had restructured your job as contracts manager to remove some of the duties that you had previously carried out. However, against our advice, you requested a return to all your previous duties including site visiting. We did not feel that this would give you any real chance to stay "on the wagon" but we agreed because you had improved so much.

By June this year it was clear that the same timekeeping and attendance problems were arising again. You were told that we were prepared to allow you further time off to dry out, providing your job could be restructured before you returned. However, you refused this suggestion. You were placed under final warning with a one month review period and during that time the situation did not improve. Following a final meeting, you were therefore dismissed.

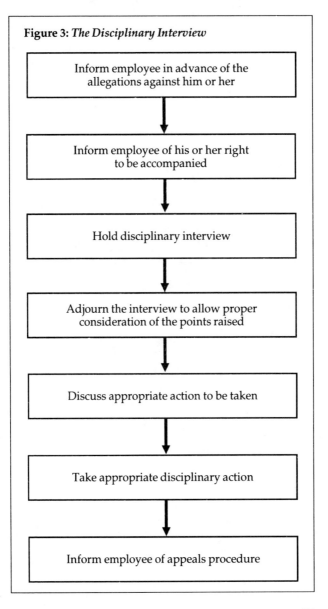

Figure 3: *The Disciplinary Interview*

Inform employee in advance of the allegations against him or her

↓

Inform employee of his or her right to be accompanied

↓

Hold disciplinary interview

↓

Adjourn the interview to allow proper consideration of the points raised

↓

Discuss appropriate action to be taken

↓

Take appropriate disciplinary action

↓

Inform employee of appeals procedure

6   Putting it into Practice

Having looked in general outline at how to operate a disciplinary procedure effectively we now turn to some specific problem areas that occur over and over again.

None of the solutions or strategies is the only one that can be used. In everyday situations, responding with flexibility and not a little creativeness will always be necessary. Mostly, the solutions err on the side of caution, and heavily reflect the industrial tribunal case law that has grown up over the years. Some of the problems covered are not really disciplinary problems at all (eg ill health dismissals) but there are aspects of procedural correctness which will be of interest to anyone who manages staff, and that is why they have been included. The chapter is divided into three sections:

● Minor misconduct including lateness, absenteeism, poor job performance.

● Gross misconduct including theft, fighting.

● Other problems including office romances and misconduct outside work.

Minor Misconduct

Lateness

Most employees are required to attend for work at specific times and are expected, with the exception of tea and meal breaks, to remain at work until the allotted finishing time. These arrangements must be specified in their contract of employment. A variety of standards of strictness exist. In some cases, three minutes' grace is allowed before an employee is counted as late and money deducted from the pay-packet; additionally, they must go to their immediate manager and get permission to start work and have their clockcard signed. In other instances things are not nearly so well defined and very often arrangements exist for flexible starting times either in a formal flexi-time system or as an unofficial nodded-to piece of custom or practice. Whatever the standards applied, the employer must make sure the standards are known to all employees. Alternatively, when advantage is being taken, someone must be prepared to draw the line. This is where the immediate manager plays an important role in tackling the lateness syndrome before it becomes an unshakeable habit.

It should be regular practice for managers to query the reason why employees are late: even check out these reasons if they seem tenuous. New employees joining the company should be told about the standard of timekeeping expected of them and that they must present an explanation when they are late. It is often a good idea to get employees to telephone *en route* if they are going to be late.

Procedures like this reinforce the habit of good timekeeping and emphasise that good timekeeping is all part of putting in a credible job performance. If employees are people to whom time has little relevance, they will probably leave and go elsewhere. However, good timekeepers can deteriorate to the extent that they need to be told and this is where the informal disciplinary interview can help.

From the outset you will need to know the answers to the following questions before you can approach the employee concerned and effectively carry out an interview. For instance, are you picking on a troublemaker? If you are then there may be some consistency problems. What are the timekeeping records of other staff? A little investigation may show that the performance of ''the troublemakers'' is no worse than a lot of others — they will have to be dealt with in the same way.

A starting point would be to have an informal meeting with the employee. At the meeting give some indication of an acceptable standard. Point out that transport problems can usually be solved by getting up earlier and catching the earlier bus or train, etc. Point out that it is their responsibility to get to work on time. Detail the procedure to be adopted if they arrive late. Remind them that permission must be obtained in advance to take time off work. Indicate that this is a toughening up or returning to previously good standards and that normal disciplinary action will be taken against employees failing to come up to standard. Don't forget to be constructive as well; suggest that anyone with problems over prompt attendance at work should speak to their supervisor or personnel officer. (Very often several employees are affected by a poor bus service and the company could quite usefully take the matter up on their behalf, especially if other employers in the area have the same problem.) Such a general warning does not count as a first warning to an individual who is being disciplined. It is a scene setter.

Are there any accurate records of timekeeping, ie clockcards, signing books, etc? In many organisations there are not, so the next step must be a monitoring of everyone's attendance for two or three weeks before speaking to them. Do not snoop. Tell them what you are doing. The purpose is to correct the behaviour not silently and secretly to build up a case against them. If they manage to improve for two weeks, knowing that their timekeeping is being watched, it is possible that the improvement will continue afterwards.

Now you should be sufficiently armed with the facts to go ahead with an informal interview if any employee is still falling below standard. (See page 31 on informal warnings.) Simply set out to the employees what the complaint is and ask them to explain why there has been this deterioration in timekeeping. These reasons will revolve around two areas:

(a)   actual reasons that make it impossible to attend work on time — eg a sick aged parent who needs attention in the morning, poor public transport facilities, taking children to school; or

(b)   the usual malaise, ie can't get up in the morning.

Both areas ought to be explored thoroughly, particularly as the latter is often a euphemism for not liking to work with a particular person or doing a particular job. Even a general health problem can be disguised here. See if there are any solutions that present themselves. Can hours of work be varied to cope with a temporary problem? Are there any other sources of help which you can give the employee information about? Local authorities keep lists of approved childminders who look after children in emergency situations. It is often useful to keep information like this for future reference.

Try to talk the employees through the problem so that they realise they must make other arrangements to cope with their personal circumstances (what about neighbours, other members of the family, etc?) because the stage is being reached where formal disciplinary action will have to be taken.

This kind of constructive approach — joint problem solving — has got to be better than hitting people with written warnings!

If there is an underlying health problem, encourage the employee to go to his or her doctor or use the company doctor. With young employees it is usually the fact that they are not used to the routine of work and need to be eased into it and establish good attendance habits. Arranging a pick-up by another employee can often provide the "knock-up" routine and incentive that is needed. Don't forget to tell the employee that the interview counts as the informal stage of the disciplinary procedure and say that the matter will be reviewed. Remind the employee that consideration for genuine problems must be balanced against the company's need for employees to attend work promptly.

Even if warnings have to be issued later and finally dismissal itself has to be effected, the ground is completely prepared and the employer will have acted reasonably given all the circumstances. (The cynical will say that you have helped to sabotage those sympathy factors that so often wreck the employer's defence to alleged unfair dismissal at tribunal.)

If there is no response to this informal warning or there is an improvement for a short time and then timekeeping again deteriorates it will be time to start formal warnings (see page 47).

Example Warning Letter: First Written Warning

Dear Mr Evans

Despite informal conversations about your poor timekeeping, lack of improvement made it necessary to hold a formal disciplinary meeting on 14 May. This is confirmation of the disciplinary action taken against you.

Between March and the beginning of May this year you have been late on average twice a week and late back from lunch a similar number of times (a copy of the records was shown to you). There doesn't appear to be any underlying cause for your poor attendance except, as you admitted, you find it difficult to wake up in the mornings. Your reason for late returns from lunch is that you sometimes go home and are often delayed by the traffic. It was explained to you that only one hour is given for lunch and if it is not possible to complete lunch arrangements within that time you should change them. As you know, canteen facilities are provided.

I stated that in future you must ensure that:

(a) you clock in at 8.30 am each day. If you are late you must report directly to me with a full explanation;
(b) as stated in your terms and conditions statement, if you are going to be absent from work you must telephone or arrange for a message to be received by me no later than 10 am on the same day. It is quite impossible to organise production schedules adequately if you do not contact us promptly;
(c) you return promptly from your lunch break each day.

The company does expect high standards of timekeeping. If you cannot maintain these standards over the agreed review period of one month, further disciplinary action will be taken against you. This will be in the form of a final warning, which if unheeded will result in your dismissal.

If you are dissatisfied with the disciplinary action taken against you an appeals procedure is outlined in your contract of employment.

Example: Final Written Warning

Dear Mr Evans,

Re Disciplinary Meeting 16 June

It is a matter of great concern to me that it has been necessary yet again to bring to your attention the necessity for good timekeeping.

The disciplinary meeting on 14 May recorded your first written warning and outlined precisely what was required of you. However, there has been no improvement in your timekeeping (see copy of record card enclosed) during the review period.

I understand that you do not wish to give up your practice of going home at lunchtimes, so running the risk that you will be late if you are caught in the traffic. You also do not know why you are unable to reach the factory on time in the mornings. By all accounts you are perfectly healthy and concerned to keep your job.

It must now be quite clear to you that your continued poor timekeeping will result in your dismissal.

I have no alternative but to confirm my warning that unless there is an immediate and sustained improvement in your timekeeping both at the start of work and at the lunch break you will be given notice of dismissal.

The matter will be reviewed again in one month's time and I sincerely hope that you will take this warning to heart and make the necessary effort to improve your timekeeping.

If you are dissatisfied with the disciplinary action taken against you an appeals procedure is outlined in your contract of employment.

Checklist: Lateness

● State precisely the nature of the complaint: what, when.

● Refer to company rules if relevant and state why conduct is not acceptable.

● Refer to excuses given if relevant and why they have not been accepted.

● State precisely what the employee should do to remedy the situation; what help he or she will receive in the way of retraining, etc.

● Set a date for reviewing the situation.

● State what will happen if there has been no improvement or the conduct is repeated again. Specifically relate this action to the company's disciplinary procedure.

● Inform the employee about the appeal procedure.

Absenteeism

Every employer views absenteeism as a cost and an awkward problem to cure and there can be difficulties in sorting out an appropriate procedure to deal with it.

Contracts of employment usually specify the hours and days of work and employees have to ask permission if they wish to take time off, to have holidays according to their entitlement or for any other reason. The employer may or may not give that permission. Other spells of absence may be caused by illness, injury (with or without a medical certificate) or exercising some statutory right such as time off for antenatal care, trade union duties, public duties, etc. Other spells of absence are unapproved and without contractual sanction.

Like lateness, different standards are tolerated in different organisations and different policies adopted as regards pay for these absences. However, with self-certification and the statutory sick pay scheme it is important for accurate records of spells of ill health/injury absence to be kept. Statutory rights such as time off for antenatal care and trade union duties must be with pay whilst time off for public duties is without pay. Holiday entitlement is usually specified in the contract of employment but other situations arise where extended leave of absence is given for compassionate reasons or for holidays abroad. Permission may also be given for Territorial Army duties, religious observance, etc, but this is at the employer's discretion.

What Days Count?

When a poor absence record is being assessed, which days should be counted and which days should be ignored? Clearly, any day when prior permission was given for the absence should not be counted. Neither should periods of certificated sick leave — the uncertificated periods are more debatable but if the employee wasn't challenged at the time it is safer to assume that they are genuine. The only days that are left are those of unapproved absence, and it is these days that form the basis for the complaint against the employee. As most employees can trot out a convincing account of a bout of food poisoning, it is better to adopt the tack of reliability rather than complain about the rather limited incidents of unapproved absence or the extremely contestable area of uncertified absence. Additionally, doctors are no longer required to provide medical certificates for the first week of absence, which could mean the dispute area will broaden. A proper system of self-certification should be implemented.

Using this approach all absence that has not received management approval, whether you consider it genuine or not, can count if your complaint is one of unreliability. There is no question of arguing over the authenticity of sick notes, whether or not they are provided by the doctor. The absences may all be genuine but will all add up, together with the unapproved absence, to show the appalling attendance record of an unreliable employee and warnings can therefore be given on that basis. Such a strategy takes the heat out of the situation; you are not calling anyone a liar and you can rely on the usual defence, "the needs of the business, in this case for reliable employees".

Example: First Written Warning

Dear Mrs Jones,

Over a month ago I spoke to you about your increasingly poor attendance record. Since the beginning of the year you have had 28 certificated and uncertificated days' absence, and three unapproved days for which there was no recorded reason. On several occasions you failed to follow the proper procedure of informing me of your absence by 10 am on the first day, which caused you problems in getting the company's wages calculated on time.

There has been no improvement since I spoke to you, because a further 5 days' absence was recorded last month and as a result a formal disciplinary interview was held on 24 November. This letter is confirmation of the action taken at that meeting.

As a result of that meeting I am in no doubt that your absences are caused by genuine health and personal problems with which I sympathise and hope you will resolve. I am glad that you have accepted my suggestion to visit the company doctor. I feel sure that she will assist you.

I confirm that you will be taking one week's leave of absence at half pay next week to attend to court matters.

I confirmed at the meeting that you must conform to the company's normal notification procedure when you are absent (a copy of your contract was given to you detailing the procedure). You are a key employee and when you are away an immediate stand-in must be sought, so please give us as much warning as possible.

Additionally, I was at pains to point out that, because of the nature of your job, reliability is crucial and unless the situation improves to, say, one day's average loss of attendance per month, I will have to consider replacing you.

You have agreed that the company should contact your doctor and we will await further information from him before we decide what to do.

The informal procedure to combat absenteeism is much the same as for lateness. Make sure employees are asked why they are absent and examine these reasons closely. There should be a clear understanding about the acceptable level of absence by both managers and employees. Ensure that there are procedures (very often they are written into the contract of employment) to specify notification by a given time on the first day of absence, when sick notes must be sent, the requirement to keep the company informed of progress, etc. Failure to follow these procedures can in themselves form sufficient reason to give warning and eventually to dismiss if they are seriously flouted.

Now that the complaint has been defined it is possible to have an informal disciplinary interview (see page 31).

Set out the complaint, namely that they are unreliable and show them the documentary evidence of their attendance pattern. Sometimes this comes as a surprise to employees because they live one week at a time and do not actually add those days they have off together and realise that their attendance is poor. Point out that you accept that some or all of the absence appears to be genuine but the problem remains for the company to have employees at work.

Comment

Once again, start probing for reasons: very often there is a sorry tale of personal problems that affect health, etc. Try to encourage the employee to go to the doctor or see the company doctor. Are there any outside bodies, ie voluntary organisations or local government departments that can help with the personal problems? Is there any action the company can take, eg vary days of work or reduce the number of days temporarily; give leave of absence to sort things out, etc? Sometimes poor attendance records are associated with alcoholism; perhaps the company can give time off to help the employee dry out. If intermittent illness is caused by an underlying medical problem perhaps the company doctor can get things moving for remedial treatment.

Where absence is caused by health problems it is important to try to obtain medical information about the employee's health.

The Access to Medical Reports Act 1988

If an employer wishes to obtain a medical report about an employee from his or her doctor the provisions of the **Access to Medical Reports Act 1988** have to be complied with. Under the Act individuals have the right to see medical reports relating to themselves supplied by their doctor for employment purposes. An employer may not ask for an employee's doctor to supply a medical report about the employee unless the employer has notified the employee in writing that such a report is being requested and the employee has consented in writing. There is also a duty on the employer to inform the employee of certain rights under the Act which include: the right to withhold consent to the application; the right to request access to the report before it is supplied; the right to see the report and request amendments and also the right to withhold consent to the report being supplied to the employer. Further details of the Act are given in *Croner's Reference Book for Employers*.

Access to Health Records Act 1990

The **Access to Health Records Act 1990** goes one step further giving an employer, with the employee's consent, direct access to the employee's health records. This could prove to be a more valuable way of ascertaining an employee's fitness for work than the access to medical reports. Further details of the Act are given in *Croner's Reference Book for Employers*.

Discussions with the Employee

It is advisable to try to establish an open relationship with the employee from the start. You really won't know what the problem is until you ask and there may be some extremely useful things you can do to help. Even if eventual dismissal is the outcome, an ex-employee will be saying that the company tried to help, but it was understandable that they could not put up with the absences for ever. If the employee won't discuss any explanations for his or her poor attendance then he or she should be told in that case nothing can be taken into account and you can only decide what to do on the basis of the facts you know. Set a period to review the situation (anything less than a month would be pointless) and say that if things do not improve during that time a formal written warning will be given.

If there has been a persistent breach of procedure the employee must be told precisely what is expected and if it is a contractual procedure then arguably it should be treated at the formal disciplinary level from the outset.

Example: Final Written Warning

Dear Mrs Jones,

Further to our previous meeting last month I am now in receipt of your doctor's report which confirms all that you told me and indicates that she has changed your course of treatment of which she has high hopes.

I have told you that we are prepared to wait a further month to review your attendance at work but regrettably we will not be able to retain you in employment beyond that time unless there are signs of a distinct improvement. As I told you, we have looked at the possibility of transferring you to another job where good attendance is not so crucial and paying you on a daily attendance basis. It has not been possible for us to find such a vacancy at present but one may become available over the next month and if it does I shall offer it to you on the basis described.

We are pleased to note that you have been prompt in your notification of absence since our last meeting.

Comment

You will note that the letters drop the strict disciplinary approach once it is conceded that there are genuine medical problems and it is clear that the unauthorised absence is because of family commitments. In general, the "reliability" approach is not concerned to dispense blame but to ensure that the employee knows how much absence can be tolerated, depending on the needs of the business.

Once again, if an improvement is not forthcoming the employee should be interviewed to make sure there is no other relevant change to his or her situation that may have a bearing on the ability to improve attendance. In this case, the interview should be used to confirm if alternative employment can be arranged and if the employee is prepared to accept it. (There is no obligation to create a job.) Otherwise, notice of dismissal may have to be given.

Poor Performance in Carrying Out Duties

There are certain problems that immediately stand out when job performance is being discussed.

● What do you mean by poor performance? Not enough sales? Not enough profitable sales; not enough new business; poor coverage of existing customers to sell the company's extended product range? Is the sales representative failing to keep proper records? Are there sales targets?

● Is it quality or quantity? Are there individual production targets or wastage figures showing the percentage of rejects?

● Is it a lack of innate ability or does the employee just not want to do the job properly?

You must define exactly what the complaint is and what you think the employee should be capable of, otherwise you cannot begin to discipline the employee. You must be able to quantify the standard required. Sometimes, the standards required are largely subjective, ie the dental receptionist with the unpleasant off-hand manner, so you have to describe the standards that are required. Sometimes it is the inability of the individual to organise the work, to work to time limits, to work without supervision, and, at more senior levels, to initiate appropriate action.

Once you have decided what the complaint is about, waste no more time. Check your company's disciplinary procedure to see what the appropriate level of disciplinary action is. In some cases, sales representatives failing to reach targets may go straight to the formal disciplinary levels. In other cases, begin with informal disciplinary action (see page 31).

The usual pattern of the disciplinary interview is still applicable to this kind of problem:

● explain the complaint in detail, suggest the reasons why the employees are going wrong, and ask if there are any special reasons why they have been unable to reach the required standards. Make sure they know what the standards are;

● listen to and evaluate any reasons they might give;

● consider what help can be given to the employee, eg retraining, extra attention or a transfer to a different job;

● make it absolutely clear what is expected of them in the most basic terms and, if there are problems, whom to go to for help. Set reasonably attainable targets with the employees;

● point out that this is an informal warning and if there is no improvement over a reasonable period of time further disciplinary action will be taken. Remember to explain the appeals procedure.

Failure to secure a better performance at the informal level must mean that formal action must be initiated (see page 47).

Examples of first and final written warning letters follow on pages 93 and 94.

Example: First Written Warning

Dear Mr Kelly

I had a long discussion with you last Friday about your failure to meet consistently the minimum sales target which is laid down in your letter of engagement. I am subsequently confirming the first formal warning which I gave you.

At the meeting you could give no reason for your poor performance but suggested that your generally low state of health may be to blame. I believe that your low state of motivation and application to work is largely to blame. It was arranged that you should have a medical with the company doctor to see if there are any problems.

I must re-emphasise that the minimum target figure must be reached every month otherwise it is not in the company's financial interest to employ you. In any future month that you fail to obtain the minimum standard you will be given a final warning which, if unheeded, will result in your dismissal.

If you are dissatisfied with the disciplinary action taken against you, you may appeal in writing, setting out your reasons, to the sales director.

Example: Final Written Warning

Dear Mr Kelly

This letter confirms the warning given to you at the disciplinary meeting yesterday. As you are well aware your performance as a sales representative is measured by the sales you achieve and the amount of new business you obtain as laid down in your letter of appointment dated 25 May last year: "You will be required to achieve a minimum sales target of £20,000 per month (periodically revised) and actively secure new customers at the rate of four per month. The company will supply most of your leads. Failure to reach these requirements will result in dismissal".

Our discussion covered the following explanations which you gave for your poor performance.

1. The products were not competitive enough and unfavourably priced compared to our northern competitor. This you agreed could not be true after you read the recently commissioned marketing report which showed that our share of the market was increasing all over the country compared to our northern competitor. None of our other salespeople has fallen below the minimum requirement.

2. Your territory was not very good because it is the smallest one. As you are aware your territory contains as many medium and large sized companies as other representatives with much larger territories.

3. Insufficient leads: this you agreed was not true once the figures were checked with the sales manager.

4. You took two weeks' holiday during the assessment month: it was demonstrated to you that standing reorders would account for at least half of your minimum target and it was quite possible for you to have made up the other £10,000 in the remaining two weeks. This is a minimum sales target, all other sales representatives get considerably more. We did however agree that a fluke result may have occurred that month and decided that you should have a further month to see if you can maintain your target. Failure to do so will result in your dismissal.

Gross Misconduct

Theft

On page 59 we outlined the concept of gross misconduct of which theft is an example. It is important for the employer to realise what pitfalls there are in dealing with this type of disciplinary problem.

There are three main areas to handle properly:

● investigation;

● the right to explain;

● reasonable decision to dismiss considering all the circumstances.

As we have already observed, stealing from the employer would generally be accepted by everyone as an act of gross misconduct, but employers must still investigate properly.

Investigation

Investigate your suspicions: what has gone wrong? Are there accurate records available, till rolls, receipt books, stock records, etc? Precisely what evidence have you got that points the finger at a particular employee? If the employee was caught red-handed, who saw what happened and do their allegations hang together? Does the evidence that you have accumulated allow you to have:

● reasonable grounds for thinking the employee was acting dishonestly, ie there is no other explanation for the conduct;

● covered all reasonable areas that would repay investigation to support that contention;

● a reasonable belief that the employee was acting dishonestly.

Merely suspecting the employee is not sufficient grounds to dismiss, but a reasonable belief after proper investigation is. If it is not possible to say that on reasonable grounds you believe your employee was acting dishonestly, can you prove disobedience by the employee, eg failure to follow till rules, flagrant breach of documentary procedures, etc?

Right to Explain

Once the investigation has been completed the employee must be interviewed and told what the employer thinks the facts are, and be given the chance to explain. Very often employees suspected are involved in the earlier investigation but when it is decided that action should be taken, a separate disciplinary interview should be held. Evaluate the explanations given. Do they hold water? If the facts are contested, opportunity should be given to question witnesses (see page 67).

There may be problems in getting hold of the employee. Very often the police have been called in and he or she has been taken into custody and charged. Write to his or her home (or to the solicitor) explaining that you wish the employee to attend an interview (give time and date) to explain his or her behaviour. Alternatively he or she or the solicitor may make written representations with regard to the behaviour, or present any mitigating circumstances before any decision is made to dismiss. Point out that if the employee does not attend or give a written reply, the decision will be made on the facts to hand and the employee will be informed.

Reasonable Decision to Dismiss Considering All the Circumstances

Once the employee's explanations have been given the employer must decide whether this act of misconduct irreparably damages the relationship with the employee so that there ceases to be a position of trust between them. Such things as previously condoning the action, long service which up to now has been unblemished, the possibility of transferring the employee to a job where money won't be handled, etc may have a bearing on this.

Do You Have to Wait Until the Matter Comes to Court?

In short the answer is no; the employer only has to believe on reasonable grounds, after adequate investigation, that the employee has acted dishonestly and he or she is as likely to believe that at the time the incident occurs as after waiting three of four months until the case is heard. The court has to decide the case on the basis that it is proven "beyond all reasonable doubt" and there are many technicalities which can cause the charges to be quashed. If the employer decides to suspend (either with or without pay) the employee will have to resume work when, for instance, the substance of the acquittal was that the police failed to caution the employee properly! It is probably more sensible to dismiss immediately following the investigation and meeting with the employee.

Often the interview will be adjourned so that the employer can consider what action to take. When the employee is recalled he or she can be told of the decision. Confirm that decision in writing. Don't forget to tell the employee about the company's appeal procedure.

Fighting and Physical Assault

The general procedure to be adopted when cases of violence break out can follow the general headings given below:

- inform senior managers as soon as possible and take action to quell the disorder;
- suspend those involved until an investigation can be completed and tell them they will be recalled for a disciplinary interview, when a decision will be made about their continued employment. Management must avoid taking precipitate action to dismiss until all the facts are to hand;
- complete investigation of others who have witnessed the incident. Very often it is a good idea for a manager to visit the suspended employees at their homes so they can recount what happened. Take statements from those involved;

- hold a disciplinary interview in which the suspended employees are allowed to explain what happened and present any mitigating circumstances.

It is important to investigate and discuss thoroughly to see if anything led up to the fracas, eg recent demotion of one of the participants; ill health; the pressure of prosecution delays; bad feeling caused by relationships outside work, etc.

Important factors to consider when deciding whether the reason is sufficiently serious, given all the surrounding circumstances, for the employer to dismiss, may include such matters as: was it really a bad fight; in a dangerous situation near to machinery or chemicals; between parties of unequal status, eg labourer and company director? Do any of the people involved have a previous history of violence and have they been warned before about violent conduct?

Don't forget to take a look at any written company rules to see what they say about the matter and make sure that in the past there has been consistent treatment of this kind of incident.

Finally, to what degree was the assailant provoked by other people, by abusive remarks, etc. Such a background may give a totally different feel to the situation. Instead of "you were fighting, that is gross misconduct and you will be dismissed", there may be quite genuine reasons for the employer to consider a lesser penalty than dismissal, eg final written warning, disciplinary suspension, transfer or demotion, because of the extenuating circumstances. Adjourn the interview so that proper consideration can be given to the decision and, when reconvening the meeting, inform the employees separately of the conclusions reached. Don't forget to tell them about the appeal procedures. Make sure any dismissal is confirmed in writing.

Other Problems

Company Romances

The starting of affairs between company employees, and very often their ending, can cause considerable problems.

The Managing Director's secretary having an affair with another senior manager may give rise to fears of leaked confidential information. The employer may be losing many hours' work if the two are meeting illicitly during working hours. Other tensions may be created with the rest of the employees who may resent or be morally affronted by this behaviour, not to mention the loss of their time whilst they gossip about it.

It is not for the employer to take a moral stand on the issue; the only concern should be if the relationship is having a bad effect on the work that goes on in the company. If the relationship spills over into the work situation then the employer has a perfect right to take disciplinary action. Possibly there are exceptions to this general approach and those would be where, for instance, the organisation is a religious one where such conduct between married persons could be considered as being at variance with the ethos of the organisation and so may justify dismissal.

Consequently, the manager must decide whether there is anything that either person should be disciplined for. Loss of time, etc, would form grounds for disciplinary action in the usual manner. Breach of confidence in a secretary could be grounds for dismissal if any evidence can be found to support it. A warning beforehand about possible leaks would be even better support for the employer's defence. More often the type of action taken is in the form of warning them not to let the affair spill over into the work situation; to "cool it" and let the gossip die down. Both people should be informally interviewed, separately, and the employer's concern stated to them. If there is a situation brewing with other staff who may be refusing to work with them, then you should explain that they should play things tactfully.

As with any situation where other employees are trying to pressurise the employer to dismiss, the employer should resist such pressure. Call a meeting and roundly tell them that it is none of their business and that you will only become interested in the couple if they allow this relationship to affect their work badly. Alternatively, call in influential employees one at a time and put the matter to them discreetly. However, if this pressure persists you may have to consider dismissing one or both of the employees to restore harmony. You should warn both the employees that this could happen and you would then be obliged to dismiss one or both of them. In practice, this situation almost always resolves itself by one of the people involved moving off to another company or the whole matter cooling down. Although these discussions are informally arranged, an outline of the discussion should be recorded in a letter to the employees involved, in case the situation deteriorates at a later stage.

Employees with a Body Odour Problem

After this problem has been brought to your attention you should not ignore it and hope it will sort itself out. Employees who smell offensively will be shunned by others and become isolated. Other employees may become very upset if they work in close proximity and could refuse to work alongside them. If the jobs involve contact with the public or the preparation and handling of food, it is a very undesirable characteristic.

This sort of problem is usually handed over to the personnel officer but there is no reason why it should not be dealt with by the manager. Indeed, the situation may eventually require formal disciplinary action to be taken and it is appropriate that the employee's supervisor should initiate action.

All the usual steps should be taken to interview the employee privately and without interruption (see page 33). How do you tell someone they smell? From practical experience, the best way is to be brief, direct and to the point; initially treat it as though you spend most of your time speaking to people about these problems. Look at the person, because looking down at your hands or away into the distance will simply offend or embarrass the employee. Try to keep a soft tone to your voice.

You could use a formula of words like this: ''Thank you for coming to see me. I wanted to have a quiet word with you about your personal hygiene. It is apparent that you have a problem in this area and so I wanted to talk to you to find out why and see if there is anything I could do to help. Of course, I hope we can discuss it now".

Now is the time to use a few settling down tactics like offering a cup of tea. Apart from the expression of surprise and discomfort, it is doubtful that in most cases an employee — male or female — would respond badly to such an approach. You will, of course, find it necessary to listen to the often embarrassed attempt to explain but the real purpose of the interview is to carry it forward and see what the real problem is.

Sometimes the body odour problem arises from not having enough changes of clothing — just one suit that could stand up and walk itself to work. After a person has been unemployed for a period a deterioration of dress can be quite noticeable simply because there are not enough funds to replace clothes or to get them cleaned. An advance of salary or wages specifically to buy clothes could help.

Another aspect might be explored and that is the fact that the odour may be a medical problem, and the employee may already be having treatment for the problem from their doctor. If not, suggest they go to see their GP.

Most frequently the problem is one linked to general neglect which can be associated with bereavement, depression or alcoholism. Probably encouragement to go to see their doctor is the most constructive thing you can do.

Very often employees will make the initial effort to put the problem right. You should stress that it is an important matter and they must pay special attention to it in the future.

If the standard drops off again and there are complaints then there is no reason why the employee cannot be given a first written warning after a disciplinary interview. It is a perfectly reasonable request for the employer to make and to expect the employee to comply with. Consequently it is an area where the employer can apply the disciplinary procedure, even ultimately to dismissing the employee.

Misconduct Away from Work

The off duty conduct of an employee may cause the

employer to consider the dismissal of that person because the conduct has an unfavourable effect on the company. In most cases, such conduct should not be the concern of the employer unless he or she can show that it is relevant to the position of trust the employee holds, affects his or her integrity or affects the working relationship with other staff or customers. Sometimes it is made clear in company rules that conviction of a serious offence will lead to dismissal. Additionally, professional codes of conduct may affect the employee's continued ability to practise his or her profession if convicted of a serious offence.

An industrial tribunal will also check that the employer investigated properly. Often information of the incident arrives secondhand from another employee or the newspaper. Check that it is the right Mr J. Smith of High Street, Dorking, before plunging in. What precisely was the charge and what was the final verdict? Does it mean a period of imprisonment and if so for how long can you keep the job open, bearing in mind the job has to be done in the meantime? All these questions must be answered in an interview with the employee if it is at all possible. Sometimes it will be necessary to talk to the employee's solicitor to get this information if he or she has gone to gaol. Once you have this information you are in a position to decide whether or not to retain the employee. Any dismissal like this, which is not related to misconduct at work, should be effected with notice being given.

Where an employee has been convicted of a serious or violent crime, other employees might feel genuinely concerned about working with the employee again. Once again it depends on the job. If it is a responsible one supervising young staff it might be justifiable to dismiss, but do consider transfer to another job where such responsibilities don't exist. If the offence is not really relevant to the job then resist any pressure by other employees to dismiss, certainly at the initial stages. If that doesn't do the trick, and the other employees are seriously worried, it may become necessary to dismiss. If that situation is likely to arise, warn the employee and confirm in writing afterwards that if relationships with other staff become intolerable dismissal will be inevitable.

If it is a question of not trusting an employee because he or she holds the position of cashier and has been convicted of shoplifting at another store, this could form reasonable grounds for dismissal, but do consider if it is feasible to transfer the employee to other work that does not involve a position of trust and access to money or goods.

If the employee's name is blazoned across the local paper for some very colourful behaviour it may form grounds for dismissal if it affects the employer's reputation but this is a difficult area and probably better ignored when it has no bearing on the job. What is news today is quickly forgotten tomorrow.

7 Summary

No one would ever claim that the disciplinary aspect of the manager's job is easy; however, we hope that, in the preceding pages, we have shown that by using well-defined routines much of the heat can be taken out of the situation.

So long as the problem is approached in a constructive manner, with the aim being to get the employee back on to the right track and not to get him or her out of the door, and this approach is recognised by the workforce as a whole, then the difficulties of maintaining order will be considerably reduced.

Periodic Review

Over time, standards of behaviour expected from employees change, as do standards of work, dress, and so on. Similarly, changes in the law may occur or your own industrial relations practice may change. To ensure that your disciplinary rules and procedures reflect these changes and so do not fall into disuse or become irrelevant, they should be subject to regular review.

Where recognised trade unions are involved they should be consulted on the changes made and they, and all of the workforce, should be told clearly the reasons for any changes so that suspicions don't arise that you are using the procedure to edge out employees without redundancy payments.

If the rules or procedures form part of the contract, then, in theory at least, you need the consent of the workforce as it is not open to employers to vary contracts unilaterally. This consent is essential in any event since rules are only workable in general if there is a broad consensus in favour of (or at least not directly opposed to) their objectives.

The following is a summary of the procedures that should normally be followed.

Checklist: Key Stages

- what is the problem? Assess the facts — including precise details of the standards that should have been reached; is there a problem and decide the standard the employee should be achieving;

- should the employee have been aware that the behaviour was out of line? Consider here whether there was a written rule, whether the employee should have been aware of it, and whether the rule has been enforced;

- give the employee a chance to give his or her side of the story; ensure you can speak privately, encourage a two-way conversation; consider the employee's replies and adjourn to consider any new facts;

- check on your company's own procedure to see what the next appropriate stage is if you are not satisfied with the employee's replies: is it an informal, formal, oral or written warning, or passing the matter on to the next management level?;

- whatever disciplinary action is taken ensure first that it is appropriate and, as far as possible, that it will have a positive effect in encouraging the employee to improve; ensure that the employee understands why you are taking the action;

- consider what effect your action will have on other employees; if a previously lax standard of discipline is being tightened up, a general warning to all relevant employees is much better initially than making an example of one transgressor;

- if the warning is to be in writing, detail in specific terms what improvement you expect, what period of time, and the consequences if the improvement is not made or not maintained;

- monitor the employee's behaviour throughout the review period; no further formal action should be taken during this period unless it becomes clear that no improvement will be forthcoming or some other misconduct arises.

Further Information

Could You Use Additional Copies of this Book?

Croner's Guide to Managing Discipline is the first in a series of pocket books designed for practical use by all those with management responsibilities. If you are a subscriber to *Croner's Reference Book for Employers* this first copy is one of four free books on key areas of employment.

Are there other managers in your organisation who would benefit from having a copy to hand? Are you currently training your managers to handle discipline? If so, why not give them a copy to help them consolidate their knowledge and put into practice what they have learnt.

> Additional copies at a special price of £5 plus £1 p+p per copy may be ordered by telephoning our Customer Services team on 081-547 3333 quoting reference CU6.

Other books

You may not be aware of the many books we publish on subjects of interest and relevance to employers. The broad range of topics covered reflects the breadth of your responsibilities and interests.

Our books always take a practical approach and are written with the non-specialist in mind. Jargon-free language, the essential facts and a clear format ensure that these books meet your needs.

Here are some of the titles we publish:

Introduction to Employment Law
by Robert Upex
Price: £19.95
ISBN: 1 85452 063 6

Protecting your Business and Confidential Information
  by Audrey Williams
  Price: £10.95
  ISBN: 1 85524 109 9

Procedure in Industrial Tribunal Cases
  by vivian Du-Feu
  Price: £12.95
  ISBN: 1 85525 108 0

Collective Labour Law
  by Martin Warren
  Price: £10.95
  ISBN: 1 85524 107 2

**Psychometric Testing in Personnel Selection
and Appraisal**
  by Paul Kline
  Price: £19.95
  ISBN: 1 85524 112 9

Incentive Schemes: People and Profits
  by Ian Smith
  Price: £19.95
  ISBN: 1 85524 041 6

The Role of the Pension Fund Trustee
  by John Cunliffe
  Price: £15.95
  ISBN: 1 85524 091 2

Practical Pensions and Related Benefits
  by Ron Spill
  Price: £19.95
  ISBN: 1 85452 033 4

Debt Recovery in the County Court
  by Michael Barry
  Price: £19.95
  ISBN: 1 85524 118 8

Dictionary of Payroll Terms
  by Derek French
  Price: £14.95
  ISBN: 1 85524 162 5

For Further details contact our Customer Services team on
081-547 3333 quoting reference CU7.

Conferences and Training

Attending a seminar is one of the best ways of keeping up
with rapidly changing legislation, trends and new ideas.
Croner Conferences and Training have 10 years experience
of running an extensive range of courses, from three-day
residential to one-day seminars, all led by authoritative and
experienced speakers.

Courses are regularly offered on the following subjects:

Handling Disciplinary Situations and Interviews

The Effective Secretary

Going to Tribunal

Concise Guide to Employment Law

SSP and Controlling Absence

SMP and Other Maternity Rights

The Effective Personnel Assistant

Introduction to Employment Law

Fair Dismissal — The 'Dos and Don'ts'

Employment Law — The European Dimension

Drafting Contracts of Employment

Managing People Effectively

Selection Interviewing

Managing Performance Appraisal

Fleet Management

Occupational Pensions: Current Issues and Choices

Developments in Payroll Management

For further information on any of these courses please contact
Elizabeth Wolton on 081-547 3333 quoting reference CU8.

Index